*When*
# FOOTBALL *Was*
# FOOTBALL

# MANCHESTER
# UNITED

First published in 2009

A catalogue record for this book is available from the British Library

ISBN: 978-1-844258-26-0


Published by Haynes Publishing, Sparkford, Yeovil,
Somerset BA22 7JJ, UK
Tel: 01963 442030 Fax: 01963 440001
Int. tel: +44 1963 442030 Int. fax: +44 1963 440001
E-mail: sales@haynes.co.uk
Website: www.haynes.co.uk

Haynes North America Inc., 861 Lawrence Drive,
Newbury Park, California 91320, USA

All images © Mirrorpix

Creative Director: Kevin Gardner
Designed for Haynes by BrainWave

Printed and bound in Britain by J F Print Ltd., Sparkford, Somerset

*When*
# FOOTBALL *Was*
# FOOTBALL

# MANCHESTER UNITED

## A Nostalgic Look at a Century of the Club

Andy Mitten

# Contents

The modern Manchester United is virtually unrecognizable from the club that existed before the formation of the Premier League in 1991.

United win league titles with a regularity unimaginable in the 1970s and '80s. There has been a transformation at Old Trafford, from the aesthetics of a virtually rebuilt and constantly expanded stadium, to the money earned by top players.

In 1992, Manchester United's best-paid men took home £6,000 a week and Eric Cantona arrived on a basic wage of £5,400. In the years before the Frenchman's arrival, Old Trafford seldom sold out. The ageing Stretford End terrace was bulldozed in the summer of '92, to make way for a new stand with executive seats and corporate boxes. Those who sat in it would witness an unheralded period of success. Off the field, United established themselves as world leaders in football merchandising.

This book is not about the present day. The photographs displayed on these pages document a time when football was a world away from commercialism, shiny all-seater stadia and astronomical players' wages. When United won the league title in 2008, the club produced a scarf celebrating ten league titles. It was as if the seven league championships won before the Premiership didn't exist.

This book proves that they did, and much, much more. The *Daily Mirror* allowed me access to their enormous photographic library in Watford. I spent days pouring over images of United – around 10,000 in all – and whittled them down to the 200 or so which are included here.

These evocative pictures, many previously unpublished, bring to life the important events in United's history: the triumphs of the first trophies, the tragedy of the Munich disaster and the successes that followed. There are revealing, rarely seen shots of United icons such as Edwardian superstar Billy Meredith, Sir Matt Busby and his first captain, Johnny Carey, lost "Babes" Duncan Edwards and Tommy Taylor and the stars of United's first European Cup-winning side, George Best, Denis Law, Sir Bobby Charlton, Paddy Crerand and Nobby Stiles.

Manchester United is not just about the players. Before the Premiership and Sky TV, football was the preserve of working-class people who flocked to matches in vast numbers. Those fans – whether queuing for tickets in the 1960s, as marauding hooligans in the '70s or dressed as bizarre mascots – are all portrayed here, as is the development of Old Trafford from a bomb-damaged stadium beside billowing factories to the Stretford End at its ear-splitting peak.

*When Football Was Football – Manchester United* is a lavishly illustrated book with a lively commentary that takes us on an exciting journey through the gripping and inspiring first century of Manchester United.

I hope you enjoy it.

**Andy Mitten**

# Before
# BUSBY

**United** are greeted by huge crowds in the centre of Manchester as they return with the FA Cup following their victory over Blackpool in the FA Cup final at Wembley, 26th April 1948.

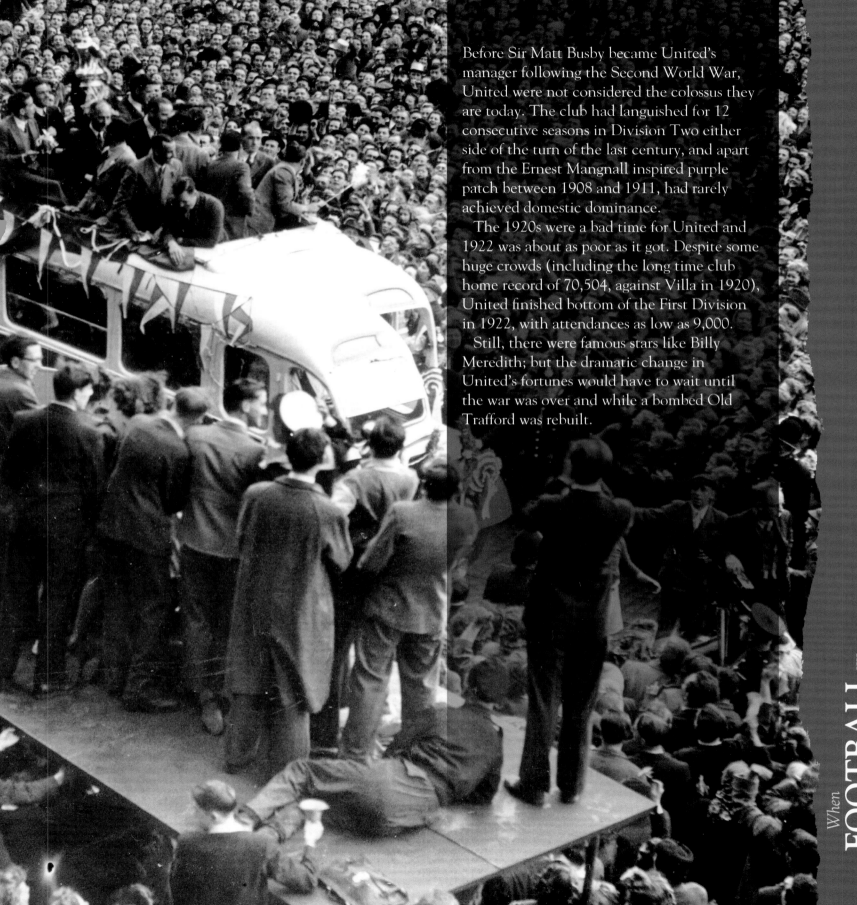

Before Sir Matt Busby became United's manager following the Second World War, United were not considered the colossus they are today. The club had languished for 12 consecutive seasons in Division Two either side of the turn of the last century, and apart from the Ernest Mangnall inspired purple patch between 1908 and 1911, had rarely achieved domestic dominance.

The 1920s were a bad time for United and 1922 was about as poor as it got. Despite some huge crowds (including the long time club home record of 70,504, against Villa in 1920), United finished bottom of the First Division in 1922, with attendances as low as 9,000.

Still, there were famous stars like Billy Meredith; but the dramatic change in United's fortunes would have to wait until the war was over and while a bombed Old Trafford was rebuilt.

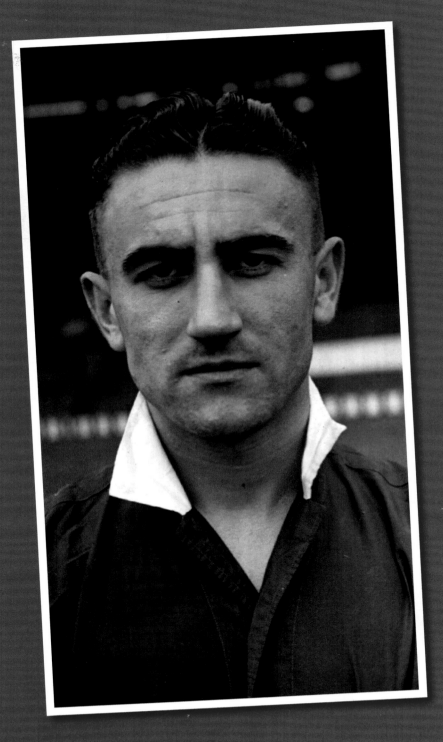

William Bryant was a Rotherham-born striker who played 127 matches for Newton Heath after signing from Rotherham Town in 1896. He scored 33 goals before moving to Blackburn Rovers in April 1900 for the princely fee of £50.

# –LEGENDS–

## Billy Meredith

Football's first superstar, Billy Meredith. One of the greatest players of the early nineteenth century, the Welshman became a United legend for his playing ability. He inspired United to their first two championships and an FA Cup between 1908 and 1911. The Welsh Wizard, who played with a toothpick in his mouth (it helped him concentrate), also played for City and still holds the record for the most derby appearances: 14 for City, 15 for United.

F. & J. SMITH'S CIGARETTES

MANCHESTER UNITED.
W. MEREDITH,
NOW WITH MANCHESTER CITY.

## FOOTBALL
# –STATS–

### Billy Meredith

Name: William Henry Meredith

Born: 1874

Died: 1958

Playing Career: 1894-1924

Clubs: Manchester City & Manchester United

United Appearances: 725

Goals: 186

Wales Appearances: 48

Goals: 11

9

United players and their wives at a function in the 1930s. That decade proved inglorious for the club. On the last day of the season in 1934, United met Millwall at the Den. Whoever lost would be demoted to the Third Division. Millwall were slightly better placed and a draw would have been sufficient for them to stay up. United had to go to London's intimidating dockland and win to prevent falling into the third tier of English football for the only time in the club's history. United won 2-0, Tom Manley and Jack Cape the goalscorers. Over 3,000 fans crowded into Central Station to welcome the team home.

# Dressed to Impress

United manager Scott Duncan with club secretary Walter Crickmer in 1935. Crickmer, left, performed many roles at the club including temporary manager. He perished in the Munich air crash and is buried in Stretford cemetery.

Duncan took over United in the Second Division and promised a swift return to the First. He said he "knew where to look" for replacements if the current United players were not up to the task. He didn't.

The 1933-4 season was described at the time by the *Manchester Evening News* as "the most heart-breaking season in the history of Manchester United". Duncan even attempted to change the club's luck by playing in different shirt colours. Several were used, but none had the desired effect.

The Manchester Derby, September 1947. The two captains shake hands in front of a packed Kippax Street terrace at Maine Road. United were playing home games there while Old Trafford was being rebuilt following wartime bomb damage.

Fans at the same match. Like many clubs, United experienced a surge in crowds after the war. Despite playing games at Maine Road, United attracted bigger crowds than City, including a colossal 81,565 against non-league Yeovil Town in a 1948 FA Cup match.

"If you glance at a photograph of a terrace in any football annual dealing with the first postwar decade," wrote historian Peter Hennessy, "you are struck by the absence of banners and the homogeneity of appearances."

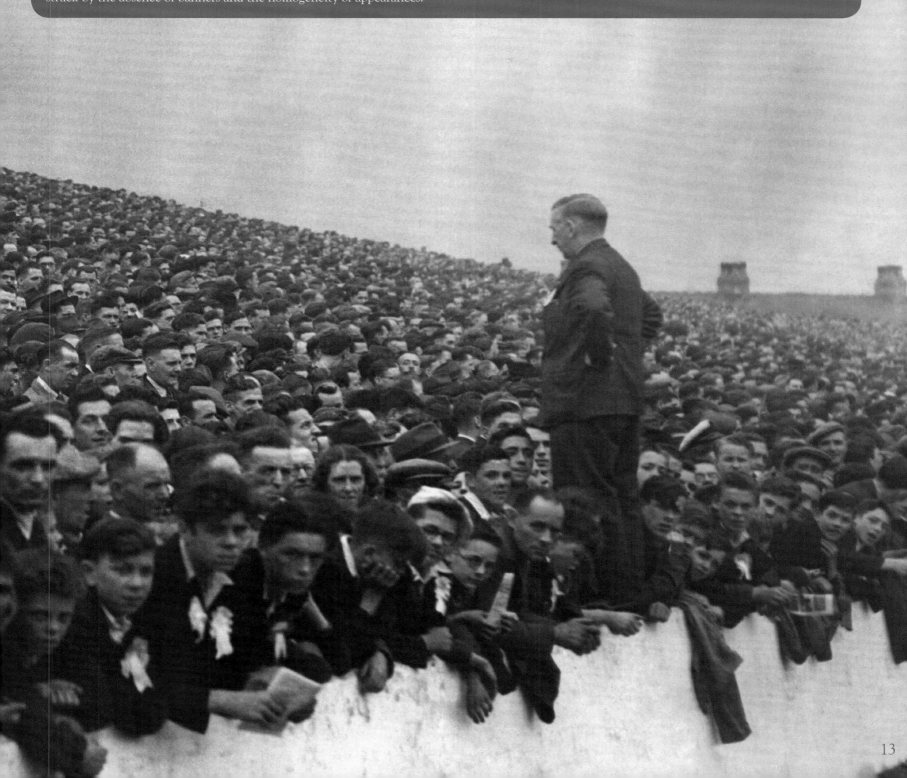

United entertain Bolton Wanderers after returning to Old Trafford for the first time since the war in 1949. The picture is taken from the rebuilt but still uncovered main stand, which was hit by German bombs during the Blitz. Virtually all the factories behind the scoreboard end have now been demolished.

# The 1950s

What would have been a glorious decade for United was forever marked by the air disaster at Munich on 6 February 1958.

Before that, Sir Matt Busby's vision ensured that United played in European competition for the first time, an innovation quickly vindicated as United showed they could compete with the Continent's finest. United were England's most successful team in the 1950s, but just as Busby's glorious home-grown Babes seemed set to conquer Europe, a tragedy struck which would crush and at the same time shape the identity and destiny of Manchester United.

Charlie Mitten returns to Old Trafford to train with United after a year in Colombia. Mitten, in white shorts, was in limbo over his future. Sir Matt Busby loved Mitten as a player, but wouldn't let him play for United again, accusing him of breaking his contract to play in South America. Mitten was eventually sold to Fulham for a near-record £20,000 fee.

Also, note how small the Stretford End is compared to the neighbouring Stretford Paddock.

Allenby Chilton, the United captain, with Ken Geddes, the golf pro, at Davyhulme golf club. Chilton was twice wounded in the Second World War, but returned to make over 400 appearances for the Reds.

Davyhulme was home to several United players in the 1950s and '60s and, under Sir Matt, they used to meet in Davyhulme's art deco clubhouse five miles west of Old Trafford for a pre-match steak. On a Monday, they would often play a round of golf at Davyhulme. Sir Bobby Charlton had a house nearby.

The 1951-2 First Division championship trophy is paraded around Old Trafford on a stretcher by United ball boys before a home game.

> " *His thunderous shooting with both feet earned him the nickname 'Boom Boom.'* "

Duncan Edwards is congratulated by assistant manager Jimmy Murphy after making his United debut aged 16½ in 1953. Generally considered to have been potentially the greatest-ever English footballer, Edwards's career was tragically cut short by the Munich air disaster of 1958. Speedy and graceful despite his powerful build, his long and accurate cross-field passing and defence-bursting forward runs made him an idol of the Old Trafford crowd. His thunderous shooting with both feet earned him the nickname "Boom Boom". Duncan Edwards's grave in Dudley's Queens Cross cemetery, with its portrait of "Big Dunc" poised to take a throw in, has become a place of pilgrimage, particularly on the anniversaries of his birthday, and of the Munich crash.

Manchester City's German goalkeeper Bert Trautmann saves from Tommy Taylor in a 1955 derby at Maine Road. Trautmann, a former Nazi paratrooper, has one of the most remarkable lives in football. He was captured by Russian partisans on the Eastern Front before escaping. Two years later, Americans captured him on the Western Front, but again he escaped. When caught by British soldiers he was sent to a POW camp in the north-west, where he stayed as a bomb disposal expert after the war. Manchester City spotted him playing non-league football and signed him. Taylor was one of the finest strikers in English football.

# Balancing Act

The Busby Babes in a training session at Old Trafford, 1956. Roger Byrne balances the ball on his foot.

In front of proud manager Sir Matt Busby, captain Roger Byrne turns to his jubilant team-mates after being presented with the championship trophy in 1956. The presentation was made at Old Trafford before a league game against Portsmouth.

Action from United v Sunderland at Old Trafford in 1957. Liam Whelan misses. The Irishman perished in the Munich air disaster the following year.

# Beating the Basques

Needing to overturn a 5-3 defeat from the first leg, United launch an attack against Athletic Bilbao in 1957. The game was played at Maine Road because it had floodlights. The Basques were the Spanish champions and the first leg had been eventful for several reasons.

The players had flown to Spain in an old Dakota and the temperature on board was freezing – so cold that the chairman Harold Hardman had to be rushed to hospital suffering from hypothermia. He missed the game and the flight home. The flight itself was bumpy and the cloud was so thick that the pilot couldn't find the runway and had to ask the players to look out for it.

The United players – with their impressions of Spain's sun and sand based on holiday posters at railway stations – were surprised that it was freezing, with snow on the ground. It was United's first season in Europe and the team were unbeaten until Bilbao outclassed United in front of a crowd of 60,000. The pitch wasn't good; it was covered in slush and mud and its condition worsened as the game continued. Bilbao had the best centre-half many of the United players had ever seen: Jesus Garay. He was so good that he kept Tommy Taylor quiet for most of the game.

The Basques were quicker and much fitter than United, and although the latter lost 5-3, Sir Matt Busby instilled his team with the confidence that they could beat the Spanish side back in Manchester on the next leg. Busby was right and United went through – but first the team had to get back from Bilbao.

There had been a snowstorm and players had to brush the aircraft's wings clean of snow before they could take off. The flight home was awful and there was a terrifying landing when it refuelled at Jersey, which saw some of the lads turn green. So it was understandable that players were nervous of flying before setting off to Belgrade a year later.

Duncan Edwards, with Sir Matt Busby and Roger Byrne, November 1957, trying on new tracksuits. They trained hard, even on a Sunday morning after a night on the beer. "They'd pound out 22 laps flat to the boards, no half-pace stuff," said Sandy Busby, the manager's son who socialized with the players. "That got rid of the ale. It was completely voluntary."

27

LEFT TO RIGHT: Duncan Edwards, Johnny Berry, Denis Viollet, Bill Foulkes, Roger Byrne, Wilf McGuinness, Mark Jones, and Liam Whelan at Blackpool, March 1957. Sir Matt Busby loved to take his players to the resort, where they stayed in the Norbreck Hydro Hotel on the seafront. They'd drive to Old Trafford directly before the game, but on one occasion in 1948, the United bus collided with a supporters' coach, which left the players "visibly shaken".

# The Rain for Spain

The Old Trafford pitch is soaked by sprinklers before the 1957 European Cup semi-final against the mighty Real Madrid. The thinking was that the Spanish would not be used to such wet conditions and United would need any advantage possible against a club who had won the first five European Cups.

United's players leave Ringway Airport (now Manchester International) for their game with Real Madrid in April 1957.

*We were a group of kids travelling around Europe thinking we could beat anybody.*

"We were a group of kids travelling around Europe thinking we could beat anybody," said defender Bill Foulkes. "Despite them being European champions, we knew little about Real Madrid. Matt, however, told us that they were a great team, the most fantastic team he had ever seen. I had to mark the great winger Gento. He caught me out a few times but I didn't try and tackle him because he would have beaten me. Eddie Colman was as quick as Gento and he helped keep him under control. The crowd was 135,000, still the biggest that United have ever played in front of. Real beat us 3-1 but our defence was superb and our trainer Tom Curry said we deserved gold medals as big as frying pans."

# –LEGENDS–

## Duncan Edwards

Duncan Edwards signs as a professional for United. "Every manager goes through life looking for one great player, praying he'll find one. Just one," said Busby. "I was more lucky than most. I found two – Big Duncan and George."

## FOOTBALL –STATS–

### Duncan Edwards

Name: Duncan Edwards

Born: 1936

Died: 1958

Playing Career: 1953-1958

Clubs: Manchester United

United Appearances: 177

Goals: 21

England Appearances: 18

Goals: 5

SAX APPEAL
The United players celebrate reaching the 1957 FA Cup final with an impromptu saxophone session at Manchester's Midland Hotel. Left to right: Liam Whelan, Wilf McGuinness, Tommy Taylor on saxophone, David Pegg (front), and Sir Bobby Charlton.

> *In all circumstances they try and play football.*

# Young Guns

The Busby Babes, champions of England for the second consecutive season, in 1957.

"The reason for their surge in popularity is quite simple", wrote the sports editor of the *Daily Telegraph*. "Under the expertly and fatherly guidance of Matt Busby, a happy band of young men have developed a team spirit and comradeship seldom equalled in any other sports. They give all they have for the club, and in all circumstances they try and play football."

The Busby Babes are 1956-7 First Division champions, and right-back Ian Greaves emerges from a wall of policemen to escape a crowd eager to congratulate their heroes after United beat West Brom 1-0. Greaves later managed Bolton, and died in 2008. United and Bolton players, officials and fans held a one-minute applause before their game in 2008 to honour him.

# Bathtime for the Babes

The Busby Babes celebrate being crowned champions in 1957 with bottles of champagne, as club secretary Walter Crickmer raises a toast.

Ray Wood, the United goalkeeper, lies injured on the ground following a collision with Aston Villa's Peter McParland after six minutes of the 1957 FA Cup final. McParland's challenge would today be regarded as a criminal assault. With no substitutes, Wood had to leave goal and spend most of the game on the wing. United lost and missed out on a league and cup double.

## A Knockout Blow

Ray Wood is carried away on a stretcher for further treatment following McParland's challenge. He would return to the pitch as an outfield player.

# Out of Position

Jackie Blanchflower, the elegant Northern Ireland international from Belfast, replaces Ray Wood as emergency goalkeeper in the 1957 Cup final. He watches helplessly as the ball hits the net from McParland for Villa's first goal. Like team-mate Johnny Berry, Blanchflower survived the Munich air disaster, but because of injuries sustained neither of them resumed their careers.

# Shattered Dreams

Eight United players were lost in the disaster which claimed 23 lives in total: Geoff Bent, Roger Byrne, Eddie Colman, Mark Jones, David Pegg, Tommy Taylor and Liam Whelan; Duncan Edwards perished 15 days later. Club secretary Walter Crickmer, trainer Tom Curry, and coach Bert Whalley also perished, as did the following journalists: Alf Clarke, *Manchester Evening Chronicle*; Tom Jackson, *Manchester Evening News*; Don Davies, *Manchester Guardian*; George Follows, *Daily Herald*; Archie Ledbrook, *Daily Mirror*; Eric Thompson, *Daily Mail*; Frank Swift, *News of the World*; Henry Rose, *Daily Express*.

Sir Matt Busby's friend, Willie Satinoff, also passed away, along with the aircraft's captain, Ken Rayment.

Wreckage of the crashed aircraft at Munich.

Six days after the disaster, the 47-seat Airspeed Ambassador – an "Elizabethan" to owners British European Airways – still lies broken in the Munich snow. One engine is detached from the plane, and other wreckage is strewn around the crash site.

> It was a tragedy for English football... they were a fine side, Matt's young boys.

Preston and Chelsea players lead a one-minute silence at the start of their game in tribute to the victims of the Manchester United Munich air crash. Scenes like this were common throughout the country. "Like everyone I was shocked," commented Preston star Tom Finney, "but more so because I'd played with a lot of the United lads for England. I'd considered them friends and watched them develop as players. It was a tragedy for English football, a great, great loss because they were a fine side, Matt's young boys."

Huge crowds lined the streets in Manchester as the coffins were brought back from Ringway to Old Trafford at midnight. Among the mourners who waited for hours was Manchester City goalkeeper Bert Trautmann.

Fans pay their last tribute to Roger Byrne, United's international captain who lost his life at Munich. The service was held at Flixton Parish Church, west Manchester, which is in front of the present-day Church Inn. A large United congregation gathered at the same church 50 years later for the funeral of long-time kitman Norman Davies, where Sir Alex Ferguson spoke movingly about the value of loyalty.

On 19 April 1958 Sir Matt Busby left Rechts der Isar Hospital to return home from Munich. Here, he says goodbye to Professor Maurer. That afternoon Sir Bobby Charlton marked his debut for England against Scotland at Hampden Park with a spectacular goal volleyed from a Tom Finney cross. The same day Billy Meredith died in Manchester, aged 83.

Sir Bobby Charlton lies in a bed at Munich's Rechts der Isar Hospital, where he was kept for a week. He was the first of the survivors to be discharged on 14 February. As he was leaving, he looked in on Duncan Edwards, who was in intensive care with a broken rib, collapsed lung, broken pelvis, and complicated fracture of his right thigh. As a result of a badly damaged kidney

United's exhausted makeshift team leave the field tired but victorious after the 1958 FA Cup semi-final against Fulham at Highbury. The north London stadium had been the venue for the Busby Babes' last game in England before the Munich air disaster, when they beat Arsenal 5-4. A young Terry Venables, watching from the terraces on that day, maintains that it's the greatest game he's ever seen.

# Barged Over

Bolton's Nat Lofthouse charges into United's goalkeeper Harry Gregg in the 1958 FA Cup final. It resulted in Bolton's match-winning second goal.

Not long back from Munich, Sir Matt Busby is helped away from the Wembley pitch after seeing his side lose the 1958 FA Cup final 2-0 against Bolton Wanderers.

Led by mascot Jack Irons – resplendent in a red and white suit, top hat, and holding a red and white umbrella – the vanquished United convoy parade down Manchester's London Road close to the rail terminus (now Piccadilly Station) after defeat in the 1958 FA Cup final.

The victorious Bolton Wanderers team had a rougher ride. They also travelled back to Manchester by rail, but their bus to Bolton was stoned by United fans as it travelled through the United heartland of Salford.

Irons was United's mascot in the 1950s until his retirement in 1963. He returned for the 1968 European Cup final.

Sir Matt Busby greets the legendary Alfredo di Stefano at Ringway, September 1959. Real Madrid, the best team in the world at the time, played several exhibition games to help United's finances after the Munich air disaster, and halved their usual appearance fee to help.

# Back to the Drawing Board

United's Warren Bradley was also a schoolteacher. Indeed, he said his great ambition in life was to be a headmaster, not a footballer.

He signed for United from non-league Bishop Auckland immediately after Munich as United struggled to raise a side. He found the move from Northern League to First Division seamless and went on to star for United's first team and win England honours – the only Englishman to win both amateur and full international caps. Bradley, who was a key figure in the association of former Manchester United players, died in 2007.

United against the mighty Wolverhampton Wanderers at Old Trafford in 1959. United's prolific striker Dennis Viollet goes up for a header with England international captain Billy Wright.

# Crowded Out

Busby and assistant manager Jimmy Murphy are almost in among the crowd at the game.

## Cold Comfort

Norwich City's Carrow Road is packed to see the Canaries beat United 3-0 on a snowbound pitch in 1959.

# The 1960s

> "
> *The holy grail of the European Cup
> still eluded United.*
> "

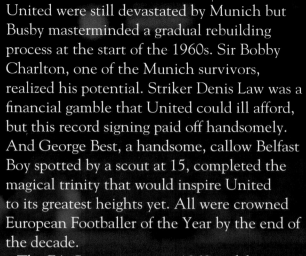

United were still devastated by Munich but Busby masterminded a gradual rebuilding process at the start of the 1960s. Sir Bobby Charlton, one of the Munich survivors, realized his potential. Striker Denis Law was a financial gamble that United could ill afford, but this record signing paid off handsomely. And George Best, a handsome, callow Belfast Boy spotted by a scout at 15, completed the magical trinity that would inspire United to its greatest heights yet. All were crowned European Footballer of the Year by the end of the decade.

The FA Cup was won in 1963 and from then on the trophies never stopped coming. Champions in 1965 and '67, the holy grail of the European Cup still eluded United. Until one glorious night at Wembley in May 1968, when Benfica were beaten by four goals to one.

> *Quietly… the closing chapters were written… to the tragedy at Munich.*

Sir Matt Busby unveils the club's official Munich memorial on 25 February 1960 as assistant manager Jimmy Murphy watches on. The unveiling ceremony was unpublicized, as it was felt that thousands of spectators would otherwise try to attend. The *Manchester Evening Chronicle* observed that the unveiling would bring a measure of closure to the mourning. "Quietly… the closing chapters were written… to the tragedy at Munich."

The simple inscription set into the stone pitch in black glass read: "In memory of the officials and players who lost their lives in the Munich Air Disaster 6th February 1958", followed by the names of the three dead club officials, Walter Crickmer, Tom Curry and Bert Whalley, and those of the eight players.

This memorial was damaged during construction work on the main stand in the 1980s and a replacement is now outside Old Trafford.

The Unitedettes – a short-lived 1960s innovation – rehearse at Old Trafford. The majorette troop intended to lead United fans in their new club song.

## Shoulder to Shoulder

Just 12 miles from Manchester, Bolton and United have always been rivals. At this game at Bolton's old Burnden Park ground in 1960, legendary Wanderers' player Nat Lofthouse is challenged for the ball by United defender Bill Foulkes.

# Goal Hanging

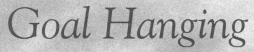

United goalkeeper Harry Gregg reaches high for a ball and ends up swinging on his crossbar during an away game at West Ham in 1960.

Former United winger Charlie Mitten with Benfica's Eusebio in 1962. Mitten became a tour agent after a career that encompassed playing spells at Manchester United, Santa Fe de Bogota, and Fulham, with stints at Mansfield, Newcastle United, and Altrincham as manager.

Here, Mitten is in Chicago with Benfica, who were widely considered the best in the world in the mid-1960s. He had the idea of taking the Portuguese champions to America following successful tours with United – including the one in 1950 where the Colombians of Santa Fe persuaded him to join them in their New York hotel room. He had met some Benfica directors while stationed in the Azores in the Second World War.

United line up in front of the newly covered Stretford End terrace in May 1962. Old Trafford looks packed, but United were bumbling along in mid-table mediocrity, and with the supporters becoming increasingly disillusioned, average attendances tailed off alarmingly. Two months before this photo, only 20,807 people turned up for the home match against Aston Villa.

# –LEGENDS–

## Denis Law

Salvation was around the corner for United. A homesick Denis Law arrived from Torino in the summer of 1962 for a record £115,000, and George Best came through the youth team.

By the time of this photo in 1969, individually both had been crowned European Footballer of the Year.

## FOOTBALL –STATS–

### Denis Law

Name: Denis Law

Born: 1940

Playing Career: 1956-1974

Clubs: Huddersfield Town, Manchester City, Torino, Manchester United

United Appearances: 398

Goals: 237

Scotland Appearances: 55

Goals: 30

# –LEGENDS–

## Paddy Crerand

Pat Crerand, signed from Celtic for £55,000 in January 1963, on the ball against West Bromwich Albion in December 1965. Behind is the cantilever stand, built for the 1966 World Cup.

## FOOTBALL –STATS–

### Paddy Crerand

Name: Patrick Timothy Crerand

Born: 1939

Playing Career: 1958-1973

Clubs: Celtic, Manchester United

United Appearances: 397

Goals: 15

Scotland Appearances: 16

Goals: 1

Sir Matt Busby leads his team out against Leicester City before the 1963 FA Cup final at Wembley. The 3-1 victory over Leicester signalled United's first trophy since Munich and an upturn in fortunes, but it was achieved against the backdrop of a relegation battle and dressing-room conflict.

"

*If we had won the game by six or seven, people would have said it was a fair result.*

"

# The Revival Begins 1963

The victorious United players celebrate winning the 1963 FA Cup at Wembley. Left to right: Tony Dunne, Sir Bobby Charlton, Noel Cantwell, Pat Crerand, Albert Quixall, David Herd and Johnny Giles.

"The 1963 Cup final was my best individual game for Manchester United," said Crerand. "The whole team played superbly and while Denis Law and I got the credit, Johnny Giles and Bobby Charlton were outstanding as we beat Leicester 3-1 with two goals from David Herd and one from Denis. I sent Denis in for a goal on the half hour and after that Leicester just couldn't shut us down. Gordon Banks, the Leicester and England goalkeeper, spilled a shot by Bobby Charlton and David Herd nipped in to make it two. Leicester's Ken Keyworth headed a goal back for them, but then Banks made another error and Herd got his second. If we had won the game by six or seven, people would have said it was a fair result. More importantly, it was United's finest hour since the tragedy at Munich and the start of a great six years."

# Crowning Moment

United captain Noel Cantwell returns to Manchester by rail after the 1963 FA Cup win at Wembley. Wearing the lid of the cup on his head is four-year-old Stephen Foulkes, son of United centre-half Bill.

# One Big Party

Police hold back United fans waiting to greet the victorious team arriving home from Wembley after winning the 1963 FA Cup final.

**Denis Law** **SHOE REPAIR SE**

**NOW OPEN**

Radium SHOE DYES

Though he didn't experience the same level of celebrity as Best, Law was a huge star. Here, he opens his shoe repair business in Moston Lane, Blackley, Manchester, in 1964.

Denis Law and Paddy Crerand in Law's new red Jaguar, 1964.

"Fellow Scot Denis Law was one reason Matt bought me," says Crerand. "He'd watched us link up well for Scotland and he had a long-term plan for United which included us two, with me being Denis's main supply line. Some people told me that another reason why Matt had gone over the border to sign me was that he considered my style of play the closest to the kind of role he himself once had while playing for Manchester City. Matt never said that to me, but others did."

The pair became close friends.

## Flying Scot

Denis Law falls over the Park End wall at Goodison Park in 1964.

# Young Admirers

United captain Noel Cantwell signs autographs, 1964. Cantwell, the elegant Irish international left-back, was purchased by United in November 1960 for a fee of £30,000, a record for a full-back. Cantwell had joined the Hammers from his hometown Cork Athletic, and had the distinction of being a cricket, as well as a football, international.

Formerly of West Ham, Cantwell was not impressed by what he saw when he arrived at Old Trafford, the reputation of the club at odds with the reality. He confided in Eamon Dunphy, then a young player at Old Trafford, "Is that it?" in disbelief at United's training techniques. "Doesn't anyone want to talk about the game here? Why isn't the training organized? What about the ball work? Do you ever see Busby? Doesn't anyone think about the game?"

"The frustration poured out of him", wrote Dunphy in *A Strange Kind of Glory*, his seminal biography of Sir Matt Busby. "He shook his head as I assured him that, yes, that was it and no, there wasn't much talking about the game."

Cantwell was the captain and he led the team to a 3-1 victory over Leicester City. The cup success brightened an appalling season where United lost 20 of the 42 league games and finished in 19th position, only avoiding relegation by three points.

By 1963-4, Busby's new signings were making a difference. Along with Munich survivors Sir Bobby Charlton and Bill Foulkes, plus Nobby Stiles, this was some side being forged. Added to these players was George Best, a product of the youth system, and United were back in business.

In 1965 the third side Busby had built won the league. Though Cantwell was club captain, injuries and age had meant that he didn't play every week. Cantwell was still captain when United won the league again in 1967, but he featured in just four league games all season and left to manage Coventry City at the end of it.

*Why isn't the training organized?*
*What about the ball work?*

A muddy Hillsborough after West Ham had beaten holders United 3-1 in the 1964 FA Cup semi-final. United had defeated the Hammers 2-0 on an away match a week earlier and were favourites for the game. Many United players maintained that they were the worst conditions in which they had ever played. West Ham, featuring Bobby Moore, went on to beat Preston in the final and eventually won the Cup Winners' Cup a year later.

# The Long Wait

United fans queue up outside the Old Trafford main stand to purchase tickets for the 1965 FA Cup semi-final against Leeds. The Manchester to Liverpool rail line is to the left, where United's station halt is located to bring fans to the ground by train on match days. The area where the fans are queuing is now a covered tunnel, which hosts a permanent exhibition to the Munich air disaster.

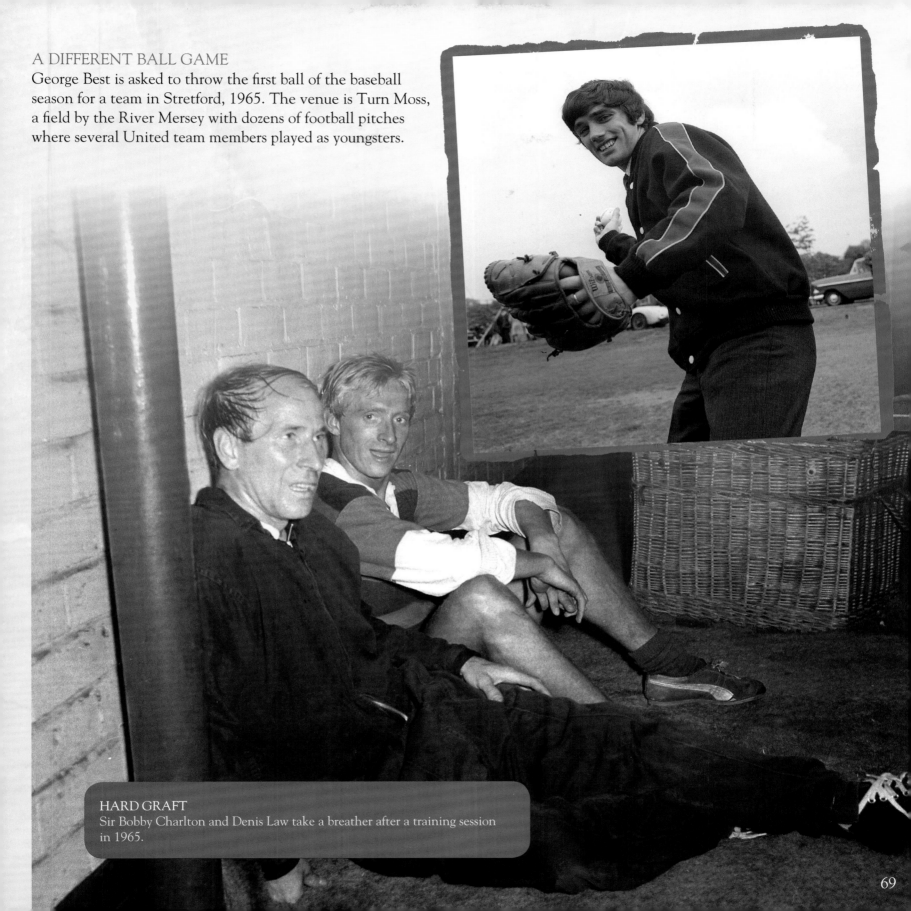

## A DIFFERENT BALL GAME

George Best is asked to throw the first ball of the baseball season for a team in Stretford, 1965. The venue is Turn Moss, a field by the River Mersey with dozens of football pitches where several United team members played as youngsters.

### HARD GRAFT
Sir Bobby Charlton and Denis Law take a breather after a training session in 1965.

69

# Schoolboy Defending

Jimmy Clitheroe, the 4ft 4in comedian who masqueraded as a cheeky schoolboy in his act and was popular in the 1960s, talks to United manager Sir Matt Busby in October 1965 in a dream sequence for his new television series.

## LITTLE DEVILS
Two young Reds play outside Old Trafford as fans queue for tickets for a cup game in 1965. Huge queues for big games were commonplace until the late 1990s, before the ticket office became fully computerized.

# Building for the Future

Several of United's first team train at Old Trafford in front of the half-completed cantilever stand in 1965. Denis Law leads them, with the empty Stretford End terrace to his right.

# Battling for Success

The cross-Pennine rivalry with Leeds really exploded in the spring of 1965, when United reached their fourth consecutive FA Cup semi-final. Leeds, now in Real Madrid-inspired all white, were, like United, battling for success in the league and cup. Don Revie's side had come up from the Second Division and were making a name for themselves. In front of 65,000 people at Hillsborough, Jack Charlton and Denis Law wrestled like two schoolboys in a playground as players swapped punches and did neither side credit. The game finished 0-0, with the referee, both managers, and players, all being criticized for their conduct.

  The replay was in Nottingham four days later, and there were fists raised on the pitch again. Rival fans followed suit, with one running on the pitch and knocking the referee to the ground, and there were disturbances on the terraces. The police later confirmed that fans were thrown into the River Trent. Leeds won the tie 1-0 with a last-minute goal, a header from Billy Bremner which was set up by former United player and Nobby Stiles's brother-in-law, John Giles.

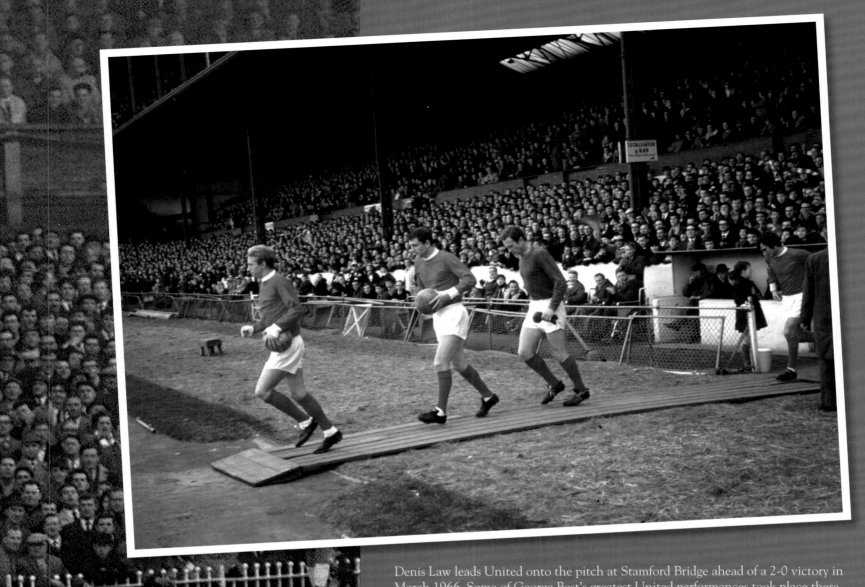

Denis Law leads United onto the pitch at Stamford Bridge ahead of a 2-0 victory in March 1966. Some of George Best's greatest United performances took place there.

> " I loved playing at Chelsea, said Best, because they were the glamour side of London. "

# Out of the Bag

The United players crowd around a radio to hear that they've drawn Everton in the 1966 FA Cup semi-final. "The Toffees" triumphed against a United side who were also knocked out of the European Cup at the semi-final stage by Partizan Belgrade.

## HAT-TRICK
Nicknamed El Beatle by the Portuguese press after he had helped destroy Benfica 5-1 away, George Best returns to Manchester. Busby had told the United players to keep the game tight and keep possession of the ball until the crowd of 75,000 had quietened down. George Best chose to completely ignore this advice. He ran amok from start to finish and slaughtered Benfica. He scored his first goal in the sixth minute, his second in the twelfth. Two minutes later he set up John Connelly to make it three. Best was 19 years old. Benfica had expected to beat United, and who could blame them when they had a European home record that read: Played 19, Won 18, Drew 1, Lost 0?

## FIGHTING TALK

Nobby Stiles shouts at Paddy Crerand in 1966. "Nobby was a great tackler," said Crerand. "He later told me that he felt threatened by my arrival because we played in similar positions and that he thought he was on the road out when I came. He disliked me because of this, but that wasn't my fault. It happens in football. When he got to know me he liked me. Nobby was bad-tempered, cantankerous and moody. And that was with his own team-mates. Nobby never, ever, stopped moaning at me, especially if I made a mistake. Roy Keane was an amateur compared with Nobby. But I loved Nobby devotedly. He was a hard nut on the pitch but off it he was as quiet as a mouse."

> *Nobby was bad-tempered, cantankerous and moody. And that was with his own team-mates.*

World Cup winners Nobby Stiles and Alan Ball stand in front of the Bullens Road at Goodison Park before a league game in October 1966. Ball was identified as United's main transfer target some years later and privately told people that he wanted to join the club. But United stalled and Arsenal got him for a record fee of £220,000.

75

# What's the Score?

An Everton fan goads goalkeeper Harry Gregg and Nobby Stiles after
United's 1-0 defeat in the 1966 FA Cup semi-final at Burnden Park,
Bolton. It was United's fourth semi-final in succession, but the team
lost for the third time in a row. The reason was simple. By the time the
game came around, United's players were absolutely shattered. They had
played six games in 15 days, including a European Cup semi-final against
Partizan Belgrade. Everton went on to win the FA Cup.

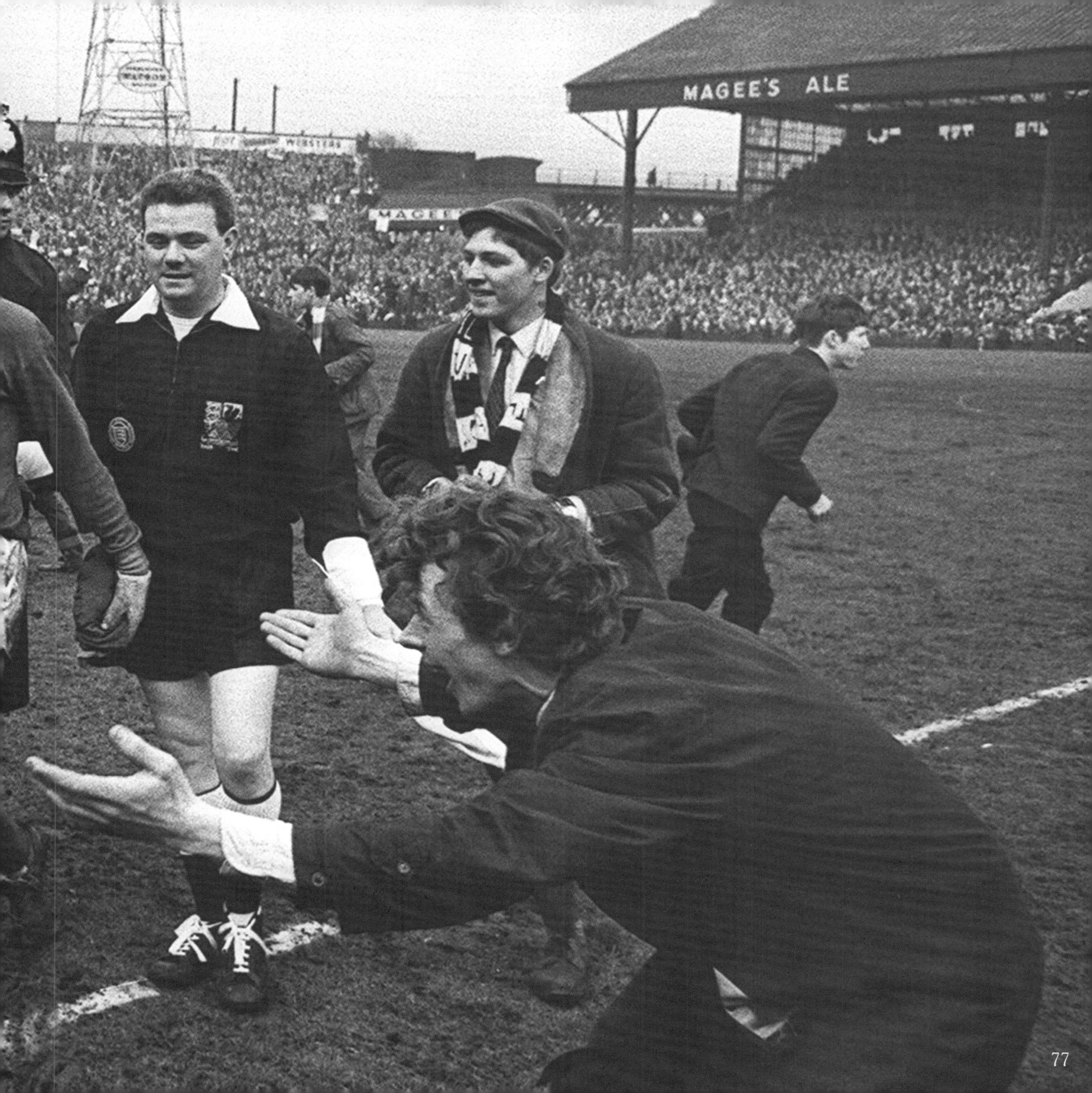
MAGEE'S ALE

A different kind of training captured at Old Trafford in 1967.

# Family Business

George Best with his mum Ann and dad Richard (Dickie) in the fish and chip shop he bought for them in Belfast. The shop was not a success. Ann was struggling with alcohol addiction and her health was deteriorating so quickly that Dickie had to sell the shop in order to take care of his wife at home. By the time Best played his last game for United in January 1974, Ann had a serious alcohol problem which would lead to her death in October 1978.

United captain Sir Bobby Charlton with West Ham and England captain Bobby Moore at Upton Park in 1967.

"There were some great players at Old Trafford, especially Bobby Charlton," recalled former team-mate Johnny Giles. "Even as a 17-year-old he stood out above outstanding players. He was definitely the top player and he remains my greatest Manchester United player of all time. Bobby was such a good pro that the things he did were sometimes taken for granted. George Best finished at 26; Bobby did it consistently for nine more years. Maybe the familiarity bred some contempt, but he has been a great ambassador for the club for decades."

# A Well-Earned Drink 1967

United's players celebrate winning the league at West Ham in the penultimate game of the 1966-7 season. The East Londoners were the team with the second highest number of goals, despite being in 16th place. United needed two points to win the championship and faced Stoke at home the following Saturday. United scored with virtually the first kick of the game and won 6-1. Not that Busby saw the first goal; by the time he made his seat, he saw West Ham taking a centre. He hadn't realized that United were already in the lead. At half-time he thought it was 2-0 when it was actually 3-0. Busby told his players: "Well done lads. Just keep it tight at 2-0." They looked at him and said, "What the hell are you going on about? It's 3-0." Busby smiled and changed his whole attitude in a split second, telling the team to go out and attack West Ham.

# Captive Audience

Sir Matt Busby speaks to the gentlemen of the press at Old Trafford following United's 1967 league championship success. Even in the days of Busby, United tried to control the media, with varying degrees of success.

Following a draw with Stoke, United's players celebrate winning the league championship with Sir Matt Busby in front of the Stretford End terraces in 1967. Few could anticipate that it would be another 26 years before United were again champions of England.

Sir Matt Busby with Prime Minister Harold Wilson and his wife Mary, after meeting for lunch at the Midland Hotel in 1967. Busby and his best friend Paddy McGrath were great socializers.

## SETTING THE STYLE
George Best and Manchester City's Mike Summerbee outside their new boutique in Manchester, 1967. Summerbee and Best were close friends, as Summerbee was with several of the United players. He even acted as a character referee in one court case for Pat Crerand.

# Sweet Charity

Tottenham's Dave Mackay holds the 1967 Charity Shield with compatriot Denis Law in the United dressing-room at Wembley. Mackay was a fearsome, hard-tackling footballer; one of the best of his generation and hugely respected by his peers. Brian Kidd is in the background. He made his United debut that day, replacing the injured David Herd. With 17 goals in 49 games, Kidd kept his place on merit, playing alongside European Footballer of the Year, George Best.

## Perfectly Matched

George Best goes for the ball with England World Cup winner George Cohen at Craven Cottage in 1967. The flags of all the First Division clubs fly above the terrace on the banks of the Thames. Best would later play for Fulham.

## Rising to the Occasion

Pat Crerand, Frank McLintock, George Best, and John Radford all rise to the occasion of a United v Arsenal match at Old Trafford in October 1967.

Striker David Herd filling up a car at his garage in Urmston, 1967. Herd was one of Sir Matt Busby's most accomplished signings. A proven goalscorer at Arsenal, the centre-forward, who was born close to Busby in Lanarkshire, joined in 1961 for £37,000. In seven seasons at Old Trafford, Herd scored an incredible 144 goals in 263 games, including two in the 1963 FA Cup final victory over Leicester City. Strike partner Denis Law got the other. Herd also scored on his United debuts in the FA Cup, League Cup and all three European competitions.

"I bought the garage because I lived locally," Herd said. "The garage took my name because people knew it at the time. Most of the United players also lived in that area, but none of them bought a car from me. We didn't tend to sell the most expensive models."

## Silver Service

Bobby Charlton receives another award – this time a silver tea service and cutlery set. Charlton, Denis Law and George Best were all individually crowned European Footballer of the Year in the 1960s.

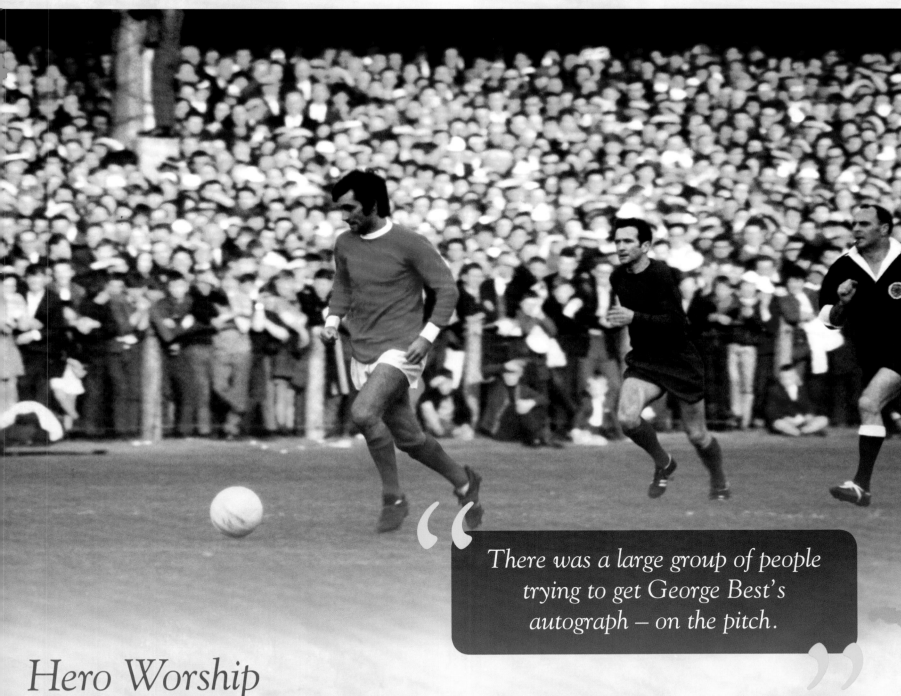

> *There was a large group of people trying to get George Best's autograph – on the pitch.*

# Hero Worship

European Cup holders United drew the Irish champions Waterford in the first round of the 1968-9 competition. They switched the game to Lansdowne Road in Dublin, which staged its first-ever football game, a correct decision as 48,000 people turned up. The players stayed in the Gresham Hotel. The Gardai came into their dressing-room before the game, ostensibly to protect them. In reality, they wanted to talk football and get autographs. There was no crowd control. The kick-off was held up because there was a large group of people trying to get George Best's autograph – on the pitch. United were hugely popular in Dublin and still are.

Paco Gento, Real Madrid's left-winger, leads the way as the team arrive at Manchester Airport for the European Cup semi-final first leg in 1968. Then 33, Franco's favourite player was the sole survivor of the team which beat United to go into the 1957 final.

# Turning the Tables 1968

David Sadler celebrates scoring for United against Real Madrid in the 1968 European Cup semi-final second leg. Madrid had charged into a 3-1 half-time lead and looked favourites to go through.

"They had run all over us," said defender Bill Foulkes. "I thought Matt would take me off but he told us that technically we were only a goal behind because we had won the first leg. Matt said that it was now or never for him and for one or two other lads who were over the hill, including me. That lifted us. We went at Madrid and they made the mistake of show-boating, thinking that they had won the tie. David Sadler made it 3-2 with 20 minutes to play."

"We were by far the better side in the second half," added Pat Crerand. "Our temperament was more controlled, our desire to win greater. But with 15 minutes to play we still hadn't scored and were losing the tie. Then we were awarded a free-kick. I looked up and hit a ball into the penalty area, knowing that we had big players like Bill Foulkes and David Sadler who could win the ball. Bill did just that, heading on a free-kick for Dave, who slipped in behind the defenders and knocked the ball in. We were level on aggregate, but there was a surge inside us."

Bill Foulkes continues: "With 16 minutes to go the stadium went quiet. Unusually, I jogged down the middle of the field and nobody picked me up. One of their players saw me and left George (Best) to mark me. George got the ball, beat about six players as George did, then looked up to make the cross. I knew what he was going to do and he cut a beautiful pass back which I side-footed in. But for a few away fans lost in the huge crowd, there was near silence. It was so quiet that my first thought was that it wasn't a goal – then all I could hear was the screams of the other lads who came running over and jumped on me. I scored nine goals in nearly 700 games so I was hardly prolific, but that was the most important one by a long way. We were through to the final."

> "It was so quiet that my first thought was that it wasn't a goal."

# An Echo of Himself

Paddy Crerand in the 1968 European Cup final. Geoffrey Green, who started writing for *The Times* in the 1930s when football was not afforded much respectability by the paper's superior readership, wrote the following about Crerand.

"Crerand at that time was regarded by many sound judges as one of the ablest wing halves in Britain if not even in all Europe. In acquiring him for a creative role in midfield Busby's judgement again hit the jackpot. The part he played in feeding the overflowing skills of the Manchester United attack in those days cannot be over-estimated. A one-paced player of steady, measured stride, he glided smoothly over the ground rather than ran. His perception and reading of the game took him to the right places at the right time so that interception and creative distribution were his strong points, just as they had been Busby's in his own playing days.

"Perhaps even Busby found an artistic echo of himself in this fellow Scot, though Crerand proved to be a quite different, a more fiery, quick-tempered player, apt to retaliate at the slightest provocation with unhappy results."

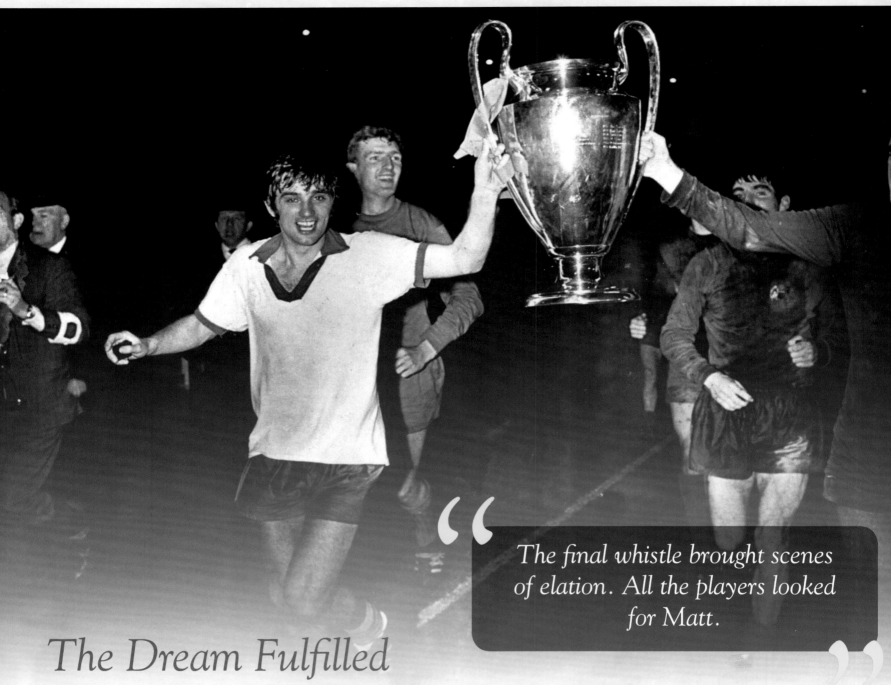

> "
> The final whistle brought scenes of elation. All the players looked for Matt.
> "

# The Dream Fulfilled

United are the first English team to win the European Cup, beating Benfica 4-1 at Wembley.

"The final whistle brought scenes of elation," recalled Paddy Crerand. "All the players looked for Matt. We didn't have to go far as he came towards us doing a half jog, half dance of joy from the bench. I was knackered, absolutely exhausted after extra time on a scorching hot summer night, but buoyed by adrenalin. I made sure that I shook hands with as many Benfica players as possible, such was the respect I had for them, but I just wanted to hug Matt – we all did. I got close to him and put my arms around him and held him tightly. He was wearing a suit and I noticed how rigid his neck was in his shirt collar. I said, 'I told you we'd do it, I told you.' Matt just grinned, his mouth slack and open, his eyes moist, almost closed."

SOMETHING TO SMILE ABOUT
Victorious United fans returning from Wembley in 1968. Most standing tickets behind the goal cost ten shillings (50 pence). Reds made up an estimated 70,000 of the 100,000 crowd.

97

> "'Champions', the United fans sing – and the players join in."

United fans cram Albert Square as the United team bus arrives with the players carrying the European Cup. Mancunians don't need reminding what a special night it was in the city. Newspapers estimated that 250,000 packed into the streets around Albert Square. There was a specially erected platform there and everyone crowded in to hear speeches from the mayor and Sir Matt Busby.

In Lisbon, a few hundred Benfica fans waited to meet their team at the airport. Mario Coluna, the Benfica captain, said, "In the first 90 minutes Benfica deserved victory. Unfortunately, in extra time, we were taken by surprise by the speed of the English."

The Manchester city police band struck up with *When the Saints go Marching In* – but the crowd chanted "United! United!" to drown them out. They also rendered the mayor's and Busby's speeches inaudible as they demanded they hold up the European Cup for all to see. Over 400 fans were treated for fainting. Albert Square is no longer used to show off new silverware. The decision, on the grounds of safety, has affected United more than the other club who used the town hall for the same purpose, Manchester City.

# Both Hands on the Trophy

Sir Matt Busby duly holds up the European Cup and Albert Square goes wild. "Champions! Champions!" the United fans sing – and the players join in.

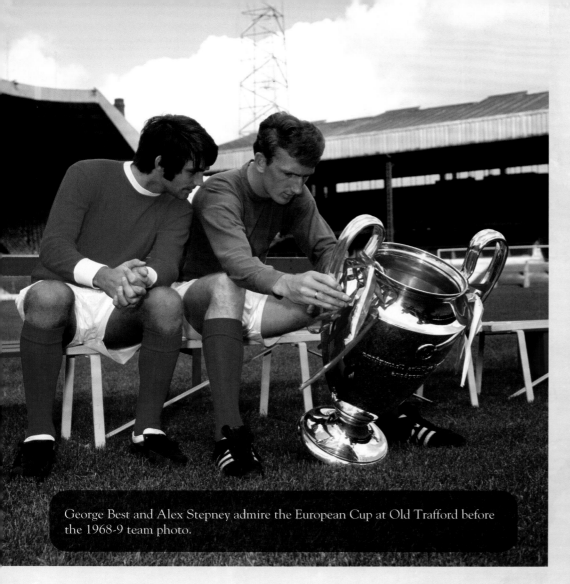

George Best and Alex Stepney admire the European Cup at Old Trafford before the 1968-9 team photo.

# A Poisoned Chalice?

Denis Law laughs out loud and many of his team-mates can't hide their joy. United are the first English club to be European champions, but Sir Matt Busby's 1968 European Cup victory would cast a shadow over his successors for years to come. It is often said that when the newly knighted Busby retired in 1969, he left an ageing and declining team. This is only partly true. Foulkes, Charlton, Crerand, Brennan, and Law were the wrong side of 30, but at 28, Stepney, Dunne, and Stiles were in their prime; Aston, Kidd, record new-buy Willie Morgan, and Best – the finest player Britain has ever seen – still had enough petrol in the tank to run for years. The problem was that the drive, the ambition, the aim of the club, had been to conquer Europe for Busby and the boys of 1958. Once it had been won, the impetus diminished.

## Red Rivals

United and Liverpool are the two biggest clubs in British football. The rivalry transcends football, yet in 1968 when this photo was taken, several United players would regularly go to watch Liverpool and stand untroubled on the Kop when there was no United game. Here, Sir Bobby Charlton crashes into Liverpool hard man Tommy Smith.

## Only Come to See United

United goalkeeper Alex Stepney collects the ball as West Brom's Jeff Astle flies in at the Hawthorns in 1969. United may have been on the wane but their pull at away grounds was immense, as another packed crowd shows.

United's players working out in the gym at The Cliff training ground in February 1969. Coach Johnny Aston stands over several players, including George Best and his own son, John Aston junior, the winger who was one of United's best players in the 1968 European Cup final.

# End of an Era

Sir Matt Busby announces his intention to leave his position of team manager after 23 years in charge to take up the less active role of general manager.

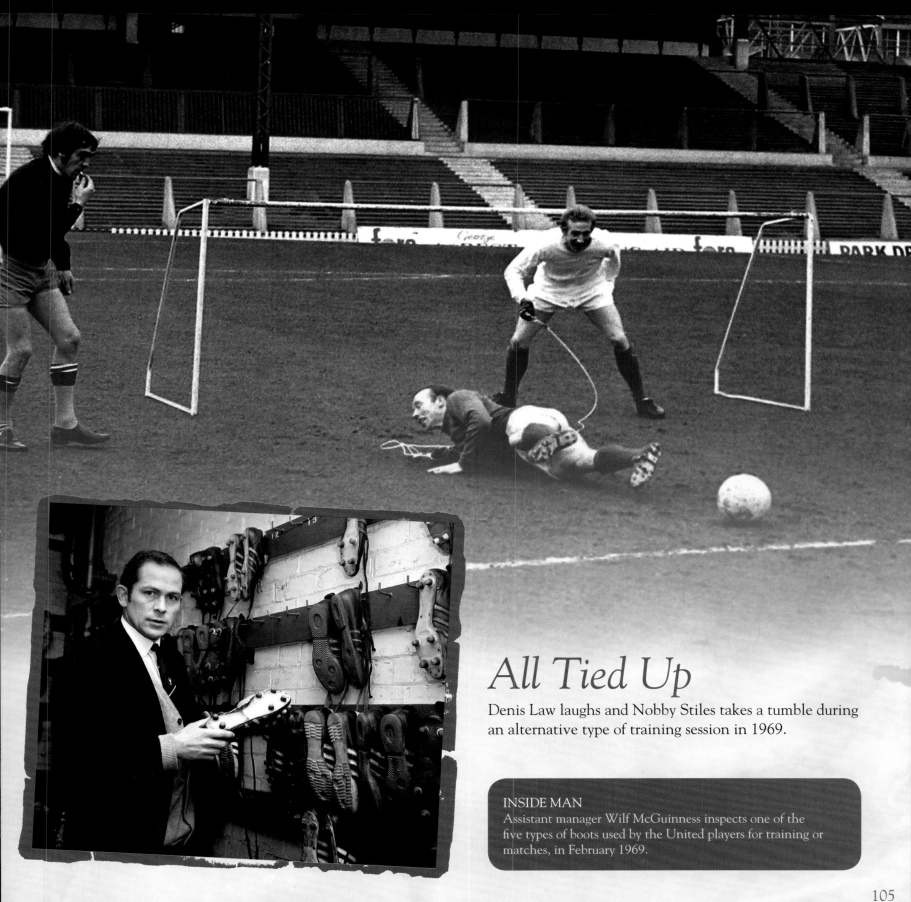

# All Tied Up

Denis Law laughs and Nobby Stiles takes a tumble during an alternative type of training session in 1969.

**INSIDE MAN**
Assistant manager Wilf McGuinness inspects one of the five types of boots used by the United players for training or matches, in February 1969.

New signing Willie Morgan at Haydock racecourse, situated between Manchester and Liverpool, in December 1969. Scottish international Morgan cost a British record £117,000 from Burnley. United's Player of the Year in 1970, Morgan was a big hit with United fans who sang: "Willie, Willie Morgan, Willie Morgan on the wing."

## Nobby Dazzler

United veterans Sir Bobby Charlton and Nobby Stiles – minus his two front teeth – at Turf Moor, Burnley, in 1969.

> " *If he had been born ugly, then he would have played until he was 50.* "

Best shows the girls of Blinkers United how to control a ball in 1969. Blinkers was the name of the nightclub he owned. Right, is his Danish fiancée Eva Haraldsted.

"A few of the lads fancied themselves as ladies' men, but George was in a different league," says Pat Crerand. "If he had been born ugly then he would have played until he was 50 because nobody would have hounded him. People criticized George for having a lot of hangers on, but he didn't. He wasn't daft and knocked about with the same people for years. Other people used and abused George in later years and because he was sensitive, he would run away from his troubles if the press got on his back, rather than face them."

107

A young United fan is escorted around the side of the baseball ground pitch at Derby County in 1969 to a makeshift police station. He'd been arrested by PC Wally Buswell for threatening behaviour.

# Defensive Signing 1969

New United signing Ian Ure is introduced to his team-mates in 1969. Scottish defender Ure was distinctive in appearance, a six-footer with a luxuriant crop of blond hair, but not many United fans today would recognize him. He made 65 appearances for the club between 1969 and 1971.

"Arsenal got £88,000 for me, still a world record for a centre-half in 1969," said Ure. "I was nearly 30 and got a signing-on fee – I couldn't get to Old Trafford quick enough."

Milan coach Nero Rocco sprays a young schoolboy with water as his side trains at Old Trafford before the second leg of the 1969 European Cup semi-final. Following victory in the first leg, the Italians were cocksure before the second game and Rocco said: "When we played Celtic in Glasgow, we went out with nothing to lose, and hoping for a miracle. The match against Manchester United is very different. The Italians and the Italian press expect us to win. And if we resist for 20 minutes at Old Trafford, you will see a great Milan."

## LAID OUT

Milan goalkeeper Favio Cudicini – father of the Chelsea goalkeeper Carlo Cudicini – lies unconscious after being hit by an object at Old Trafford. United were chasing a 2-0 defeat from the first leg.

Cudicini hadn't conceded more than two goals in a game for two years and Milan were ready for United. They had players like Gianni Rivera, who succeeded George Best as the European Footballer of the Year. The Italians had two very good chances in the first half, which, if converted, would have killed the tie. Just before half-time, a misguided United fan threw something from the crowd, which hit Cudicini.

In front of a crowd of 63,000, United played well and came close to scoring four times in the first half, but it took until the 70th minute before Sir Bobby Charlton put the team ahead. The French referee Machin disallowed a perfectly good Denis Law shot which crossed the line, and United ended up going out 2-1 on aggregate. Milan destroyed Ajax 4-0 in the final in Madrid.

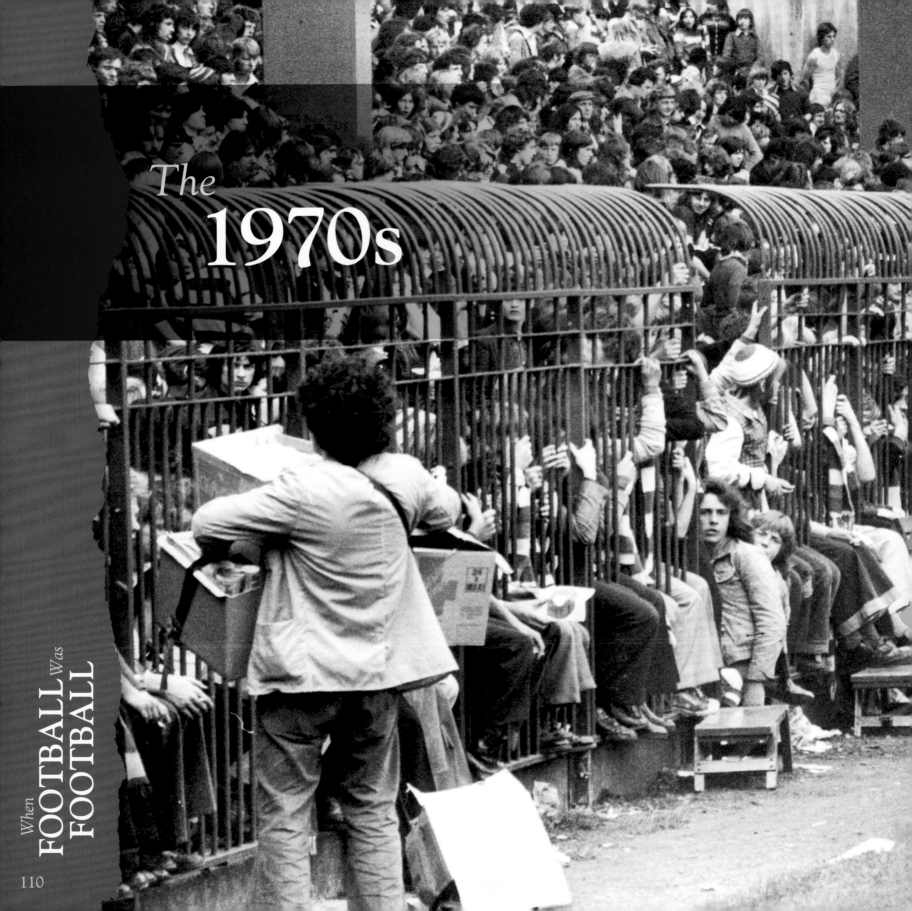

The
# 1970s

Decline had set in after the European success in '68. An ageing team needed rebuilding and Sir Matt Busby, understandably, with nothing left to prove was not the man to oversee the building of a fourth side under his tutelage. By the early '70s, Busby had departed and a succession of likely and, some very unlikely, suitors followed: Wilf McGuinness, Frank O'Farrell, Tommy Docherty and Dave Sexton.

All made their imprint on United's history, as did the club's burgeoning support – though not always for the right reasons. While the noise at the Stretford End was measured to equal that of a 747 at take off, hooliganism saw fences erected at Old Trafford. The fans, caged-in like animals, saw it all in the '70s, fashions, fandom and football that remain unique to that decade.

## George Best

George Best referred to his new specially commissioned house as his "Saturn Five Space Station House". Fans used to besiege the property near Bramhall in the early 1970s and play football on the lawn outside, which didn't please his gardener, who also happened to be a United groundsman. Architectural critics claimed the house looked like a public lavatory from the outside. Inside, the lavish furnishings consisted of the copious use of marble, full-length tinted windows – and plenty of female visitors.

## FOOTBALL –STATS–

### George Best

Name: George Best

Born: 1946

Died: 2005

Playing Career: 1963-1984

Clubs: Manchester United, Dunstable Town, Stockport County, Cork Celtic, Los Angeles Aztec, Fulham, Fort Lauderdale Strikers, San Jose Earthquakes, Bournemouth, Brisbane Lions, Tobermore United

United Appearances: 470

Goals: 179

Northern Ireland Appearances: 37

Goals: 9

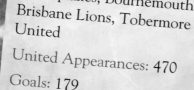

George Best is surrounded by photographers after being sent off against Arsenal at Highbury in 1970.

> *Best used to pretend to listen to Matt, while at the same time counting the flowers on the wallpaper in his office.*

## Off the Rails

Sir Matt Busby, with his QE2 luxury liner suit bag, and George Best return to Manchester after Best's sending off at Chelsea in 1971. No matter how hard he tried, Busby couldn't get Best to alter his lifestyle. Whatever promises George made were never kept. Best used to pretend to listen to Matt, while at the same time counting the flowers on the wallpaper in his office.

Pat Crerand, Willie Morgan, and John Aston are fully kitted out for the team photo of the 1971-2 season at Old Trafford. Behind them, 'K' Stand is being constructed.

# Salute to the King

The Stretford End's demon "King", Denis Law, was adored by the Old Trafford faithful for his potent marksmanship and abrasive impudence. Lean and lion-haired, the Scot was an explosive force in front of goal, combining razor-sharp reflexes and an acrobatic athleticism with a powerful shot, speed and irrepressible cheek. "No other player," noted Sir Matt Busby, "scores as many miracle goals as Denis. He's the quickest-thinking player I've ever seen." Never afraid to stand up for himself on the pitch, Law was an unrepentant avenger of fouls committed against him, who frequently came into conflict with the authorities, who handed him a series of draconian punishments. A statue, immortalizing Law's trademark goal celebration – sleeve cuffs pulled down over his hands, ends clutched between his fingers, one arm raised in salute with finger pointing to the sky – stands in the Stretford End concourse.

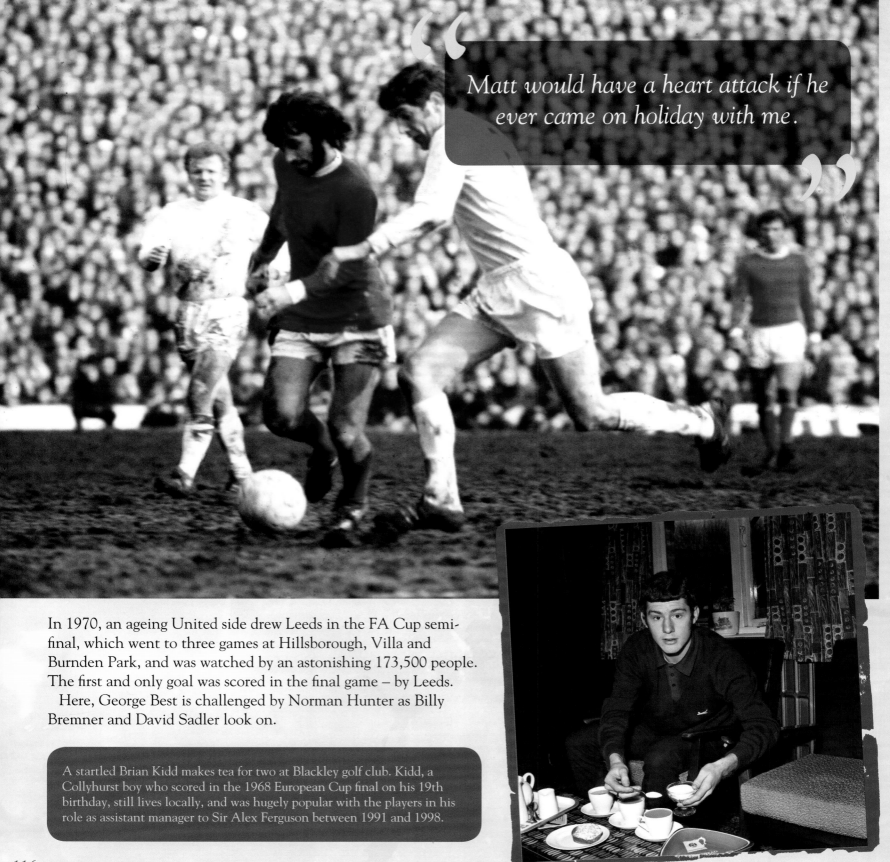

"Matt would have a heart attack if he ever came on holiday with me."

In 1970, an ageing United side drew Leeds in the FA Cup semi-final, which went to three games at Hillsborough, Villa and Burnden Park, and was watched by an astonishing 173,500 people. The first and only goal was scored in the final game – by Leeds.

Here, George Best is challenged by Norman Hunter as Billy Bremner and David Sadler look on.

A startled Brian Kidd makes tea for two at Blackley golf club. Kidd, a Collyhurst boy who scored in the 1968 European Cup final on his 19th birthday, still lives locally, and was hugely popular with the players in his role as assistant manager to Sir Alex Ferguson between 1991 and 1998.

Best on holiday in Palma Nova, Majorca, with his girlfriend, the actress Susan George. "Matt would have a heart attack if he ever came on holiday with me," said Best. "I used to go to Majorca and Spain because all the Scandinavian crumpet went there and I am very partial to Scandinavian crumpet, it generally being beautiful, always willing and a bit thick so you don't have to waste time with the conversation."

# -LEGENDS-

## Sir Bobby Charlton

A footballing institution, Sir Bobby Charlton's worldwide reputation for sportsmanship has brought honour and dignity to Manchester United and English football in general. However, his immense contribution to United's footballing success should not be overshadowed by his achievements as a football ambassador, for which he was knighted in 1994. When he first broke into the Manchester United team, as one of the Busby Babes, he was often used as a left-winger to take advantage of his blistering sprinter's pace, beating his man for speed but also with his body swerve, feinting to the left then suddenly veering to the right.

The most elegant and exhilarating of runners, he glided over the ground. Later, playing in a more central role, he employed perfectly placed long passes to devastating effect. Most thrilling of all for spectators was his bullet shot, low and hard, achieved with virtually no backlift. He still holds the English international goalscoring record. After surviving the Munich air crash, he became a symbol of the club's regeneration and was a mainstay of the team for 17 years. He has also served United as a director for many years.

## FOOTBALL -STATS-

### Sir Bobby Charlton

Name: Sir Robert Charlton

Born: 1937

Playing Career: 1954-1975

Clubs: Manchester United, Preston North End, Waterford United

United Appearances: 759

Goals: 249

England Appearances: 106

Goals: 49

Ipswich full-back Mick Mills prepares to hammer George Best ahead of a 1970 Cup tie at Portman Road. United won.

Wilf McGuiness, Sir Matt Busby's replacement as United manager, on the Old Trafford pitch in July 1970. "Matt had tremendous vision appointing someone from within the club, that hadn't been done before," said winger Willie Morgan. "The idea was right, but it just didn't work out. Wilf's a great bloke now, but he was just too immature, too petty and he messed up."

Frank O'Farrell was next, having been appointed in July 1971. The urbane Irishman from Cork had been a success at Leicester City, but he felt constantly undermined by Busby at Old Trafford.

"Old Trafford was big," recollected O'Farrell of his initial encounter in this photo. "I was impressed by the size of the place." It was on this first day that O'Farrell decided to grasp his first nettle. "Matt's office was the manager's office," explained O'Farrell. "He said that a new office was being built for the new manager. I was uneasy with that and said to Matt: 'Before I came here the press were speculating that no one would come here because you would still be here. It will be symbolic if I don't use what is regarded as the manager's office.' I said it in a polite way and I had to say it. I was impressed by him but I wasn't overawed and I was confident myself. Matt relented and moved his stuff out."

Pat Crerand in 1971. This photo was used as the cover to *Never Turn the Other Cheek*, his 2007 autobiography. Always combative on and off the field, Crerand has been a popular, if outspoken, mainstay among United pundits since the early 1990s.

OUR KIDD: Brian Kidd against Everton at Goodison Park, with its new main stand, in 1972. After a great career, Kidd returned to United to train the youth team in 1989. He was instrumental in scouting many of the players who formed the celebrated "Class of '92". By 1991 he was assistant manager and helped United win plenty of events: the league in 1993, '94, '96, and '97, and the FA Cup in 1994 and '96. The side he left when he moved to manage Blackburn in December 1998 won the treble. The United players who worked under him still adore him.

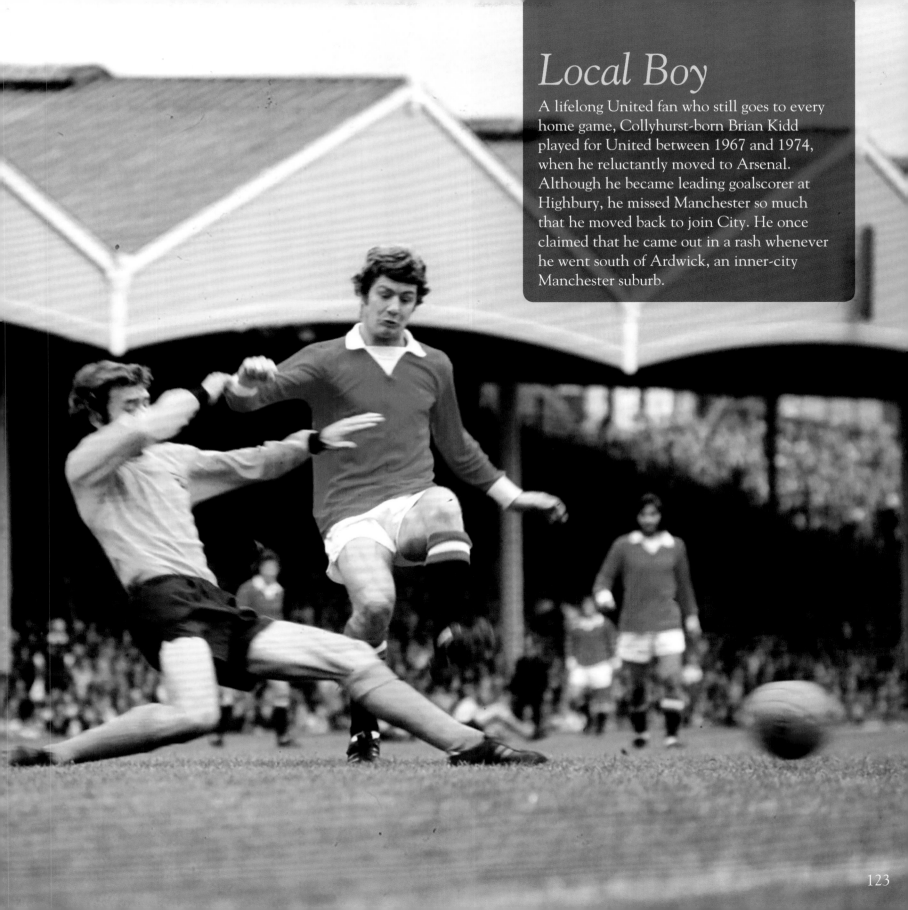

## Local Boy

A lifelong United fan who still goes to every home game, Collyhurst-born Brian Kidd played for United between 1967 and 1974, when he reluctantly moved to Arsenal. Although he became leading goalscorer at Highbury, he missed Manchester so much that he moved back to join City. He once claimed that he came out in a rash whenever he went south of Ardwick, an inner-city Manchester suburb.

The Stretford End, January 1971, for an FA Cup third-round tie against Middlesbrough. Because of troublesome fans and objects thrown at visiting players, the central section of the terrace behind the goal was closed.

The bench, Old Trafford, 1971. Manager and players now sit in a slightly elevated position, even closer to the supporters behind.

Crowds gather outside Old Trafford before United's league game against Derby County in September 1972. The floodlights were taken down in 1987 and replaced by lights in the new main stand. The old brick stand was gradually replaced in the early 1980s so that it matched up with the newer 'K' Stand, to the right of the picture, in 1985.

# Public Address

Frank O'Farrell was fond of addressing his players on the pitch at The Cliff. Here, the United squad model the male fashions of the day.

United manager Frank O'Farrell, former manager Sir Matt Busby, Sir Bobby Charlton and chairman Louis Edwards, plus their wives, are among the guests for a gala dinner in Manchester in 1972.

"At one club function Matt said to my wife after a few drinks: 'Your husband is an independent sod, why don't you get him to talk to me?'" said O'Farrell. "I invited Matt for a coffee in my office the following Monday, as I did most Mondays. I didn't sit at my desk and look down at him or anything like that, but I told him what he had said to my wife.

"Matt mumbled on before saying: 'I didn't think you should have dropped Bobby Charlton.' With that Matt was interfering with my team. He also said, 'I don't think Martin Buchan is playing so well.' He was picking on Martin Buchan who wasn't playing badly at all. From then on it was only a matter of time before the situation disintegrated. He shouldn't have gone to my wife."

## PANIC BUY

United's slide began almost as soon as the club won the European Cup in 1968. United finished 11th, 8th, and 8th in successive seasons and, in 1972-3, 18th. By that time, the team was an ageing and transitional one, which failed to register a win until the 10th league game of the season.

No fewer than 11 players had their last games for United in 1972-3, including two main talents of the previous decade, Bobby Charlton and Denis Law. Another, George Best, was at his most troublesome thanks to his extra-curricular excesses, and his contract was terminated by "mutual agreement".

Stuck at the foot of the First Division, the chequebook was produced to buy the previously free-scoring McDougall from Bournemouth for £200,000, and Wyn Davies from Manchester City for £65,000. Neither could arrest the poor form, and neither lasted more than a few months at a troubled Old Trafford. Following a 5-0 thrashing away at Crystal Palace in December, genial O'Farrell was dismissed.

129

# Calling the Tune

Scotland manager Tommy Docherty took over from O'Farrell, lavishing money and making drastic changes. He would bring in no fewer than six Scottish players: George Graham, Alex Forsyth, Lou Macari, Jim Holton, Stewart Houston, and Jim McCalliog, as well as others. The new players breathed life into the club and a spring revival saw United avoid relegation by finishing 18th.

But there was little salvation in the cups in one of United's worst seasons. Wolves knocked United out of the FA Cup in the third round and Bristol Rovers did likewise in the league cup, winning 2-1 at Old Trafford.

New United manager Tommy Docherty with Denis Law and David Sadler in 1973. United would go down before Docherty turned things around. Unfortunately, his relationship with Law soured and the original King of the Stretford End left United, discarded on a free transfer to City.

The flag says it all as Old Trafford welcomes back Nobby Stiles, wearing the unfamiliar colours of Middlesbrough's away kit, returning for the first time since his transfer to Ayresome Park.

Sir Bobby Charlton is consoled by Peter Bonetti as he leaves the pitch after playing his final game for United at Stamford Bridge in April 1973. Charlton played 759 times for United, a club record which stood until Ryan Giggs eclipsed it in 2008.

Sir Bobby Charlton puts his head in his hands and cries as he realizes that he's the star of television's *This Is Your Life* in 1969. Presenter Eamonn Andrews recites his life and Sir Matt Busby looks on with a smile.

"Six foot two, eyes of blue," sang Reds about the former defender Jim Holton, seen here playing at Chelsea in 1973, "Big Jim Holton's after you." Except he had brown eyes and was 6ft 1in.

The people on the packed terraces of the Shelf at White Hart Lane watch on as United's long-time goalkeeper Alex Stepney makes a spectacular flying save in a league defeat to Tottenham in March 1972.

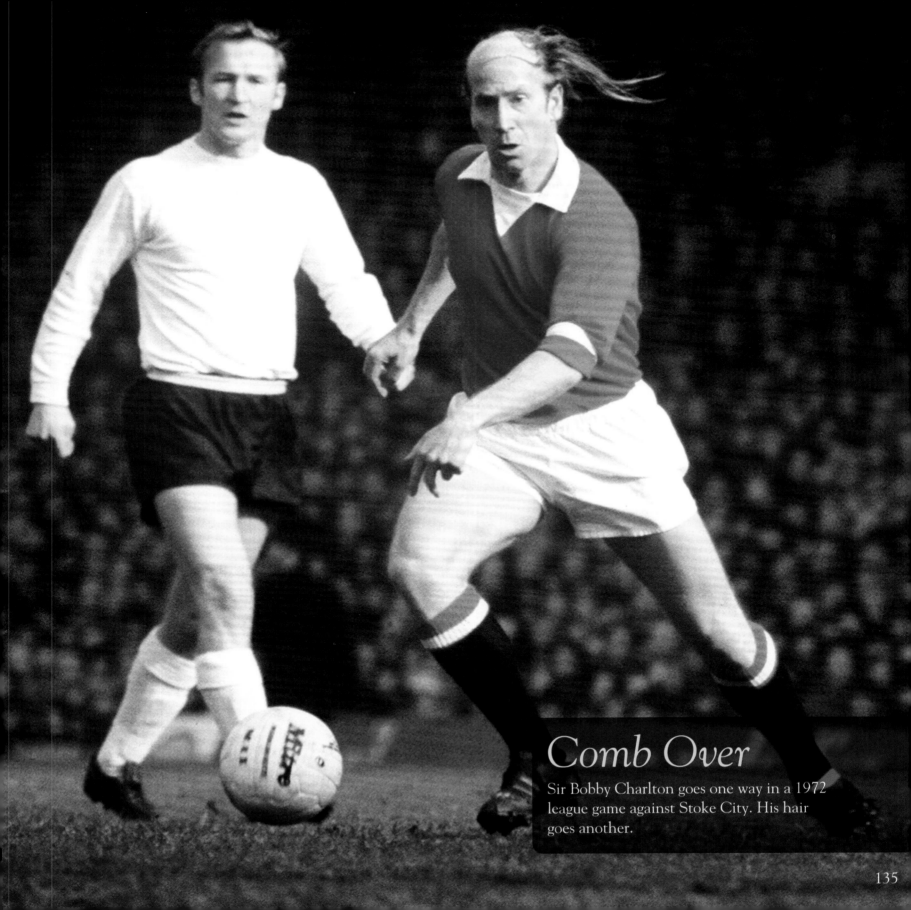

# Comb Over

Sir Bobby Charlton goes one way in a 1972 league game against Stoke City. His hair goes another.

## High Roller

George Best arrives for a training session at
Old Trafford in his new Rolls-Royce, 1972.

## NOT YOUR ARCHETYPAL FOOTBALLER

"Martin Buchan wasn't your archetypal professional," said Frank Stapleton. "He was well respected as captain. He liked things to be done in a certain way – apprentices had to knock on the door of the first-team dressing-room at the training ground for example. On a match day he liked to be in control, but he was a good club man and he liked being at United. He was a very good player, a solid, quick, efficient if not spectacular defender. I can't remember Kenny Dalglish getting the better of him too many times. Martin had a wicked sense of humour. He would start laughing at his own joke before he had told the punch line.

"He was starting to be edged out at United when I was there so he moved after getting a two-year contract under Joe Royle at Oldham. Martin was very principled. At the end of his first year at Oldham, he said to Joe, 'I can't keep doing this and taking your money. I don't think I'm justifying myself and would like to close it here.' He retired and walked away from the security of a one-year contract."

# Making Waves

George Best alone on a Spanish beach in 1972. In the spring of 1972, Best decided to quit football and go and live in Spain. Best didn't live like a professional, but he played like one and was United's top scorer five seasons in a row. Seventeen days later, George returned to United, having decided to come out of 'retirement'.

# Divided Loyalties

Denis Law's last kick in football – a back-heeled goal for City against United at Old Trafford in April 1974; a goal he didn't celebrate. It's remembered as the goal that sent United down, but other results ensured that United were already relegated. The only thing that pleased Denis about that goal was the damage it caused Tommy Docherty.

Oxford fans flee from the fearsome Red Army outside the tiny Manor Ground after the game.

"There were times when it kicked off and fans spilled onto the pitch," recalled former striker Stuart Pearson, "but the players never felt in danger because away grounds were always full of our own fans. We'd have a chat and the fans would listen. Often, problems arose because there were so many fans packed into a confined area that the terrace would break its bank like a swollen river."

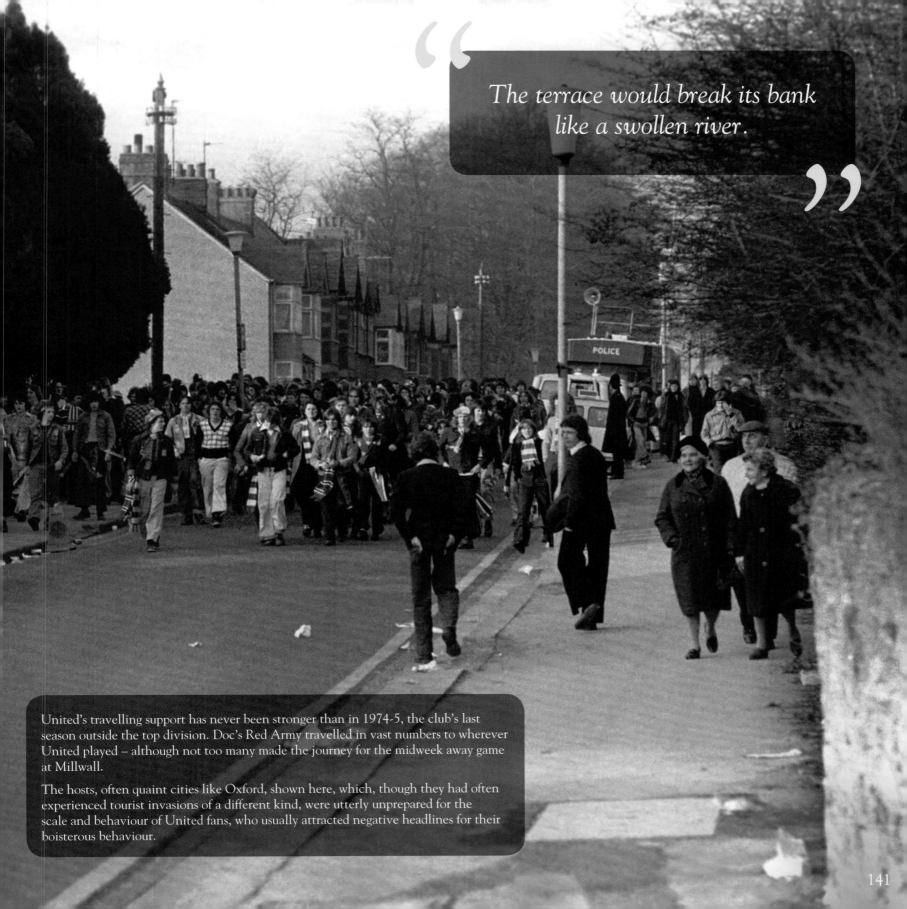

> "The terrace would break its bank like a swollen river."

United's travelling support has never been stronger than in 1974-5, the club's last season outside the top division. Doc's Red Army travelled in vast numbers to wherever United played – although not too many made the journey for the midweek away game at Millwall.

The hosts, often quaint cities like Oxford, shown here, which, though they had often experienced tourist invasions of a different kind, were utterly unprepared for the scale and behaviour of United fans, who usually attracted negative headlines for their boisterous behaviour.

As in a zoo, in 1974 United were ordered to cage fans in by installing 8ft-high fences. The order came from an FA commission after a pitch invasion late in the match against Manchester City in the relegation season of 1973-4, which saw the game abandoned and City awarded the points.

They were used for the first time here in August 1974, with United in the Second Division. The fences stayed until the early 1990s when they were gradually reduced in size and then demolished altogether.

## Bouncing Back

United captain Martin Buchan and goalkeeper Alex Stepney parade the 1974-5 Second Division championship trophy around Old Trafford.

In the deciding match, manager Tommy Docherty went for a system using wide men, with Steve Coppell and Gordon Hill rampaging down the wings. With Lou Macari and Sammy McIlroy scuttling around the middle and Martin Buchan solid in defence, United bounced back at the first attempt. Goalkeeper Alex Stepney, by now the only survivor of 1968, kept his reputation intact with a great season.

Signed up from Hull for £200,000 in 1973, Stuart Pearson was United's joint top league scorer in both 1975-6 and 1976-7. Hugely popular with fans, in part because of his clenched-fist goal salute, Reds sang: "I'd walk a million miles for one of your goals…"

Pearson loved his time at Old Trafford. "It sounds daft but most of us were best mates," he said. "We'd drink in the Little B pub in Sale, where most of the players lived. And each weekday we'd go for lunch to Oscars, Bestie's place in town. We'd not drink alcohol though; we just had a laugh together. We played golf twice a week too."

United's stars record their 1976 FA Cup final song, called *Manchester United*. Tommy Docherty's first Cup final squad stated the obvious: "We're Manchester United, Manchester United, / So come along and join in our fight." Some of the Red Army took this literally. The B side is captain Martin Buchan's self-penned *Old Trafford Blues*: "Then there's Alex Stepney, the grandad of the team, / He's been playing football since 1917."

Southampton manager Lawrie McMenemy (left) and United boss Tommy Docherty (brown trousers) lead their sides out for the 1976 FA Cup final.

## Plastered

George Best is gagged for a 1976 photo shoot, a shame because his comments were often worth reading.

"I always saw myself as an entertainer," he often said. "It was my job to go out there and give them a show."

> " *I always saw myself as an entertainer.* "

# Back Where They Belong

The United team line up for their pre-season team photo in July 1976. It would be a good season for the Reds.

"I watched the 1975 final as a student and a year later I was playing in it," said United winger Steve Coppell. "I didn't feel that bad after the game but later it dawned that it might be the only time I played in a cup final and I got really depressed.

"After the defeat the Doc told fans: 'We're going to win the cup for you next year.' All the players thought, 'Oh, no', but we did win – and against a team chasing the treble."

Liverpool, to be precise, Coppell's childhood favourite.

Lou Macari and Jimmy Greenhoff celebrate as United go 2-1 up against a treble-chasing Liverpool in the 1977 FA Cup final at Wembley.

"I had plenty of good times at United," said Macari, who made 404 appearances for the club and scored 97 goals, "the highlight being when my shot deflected off Jimmy Greenhoff to win the FA Cup final against Liverpool."

The 1970s saw United fans explode into colour – and some rather questionable attire. White butcher coats covered in United badges were fashionable, as was having two bar scarves tied around your wrists. Here, United fans are in good mood before the 1977 FA Cup final against Liverpool.

# A Promise Kept

Sammy McIlroy holds the lid of the FA Cup trophy, while Stuart Pearson and Steve Coppell clutch the cup after defeating Liverpool in the hot May sunshine. Most of the United players in that team describe that day as the highlight of their careers.

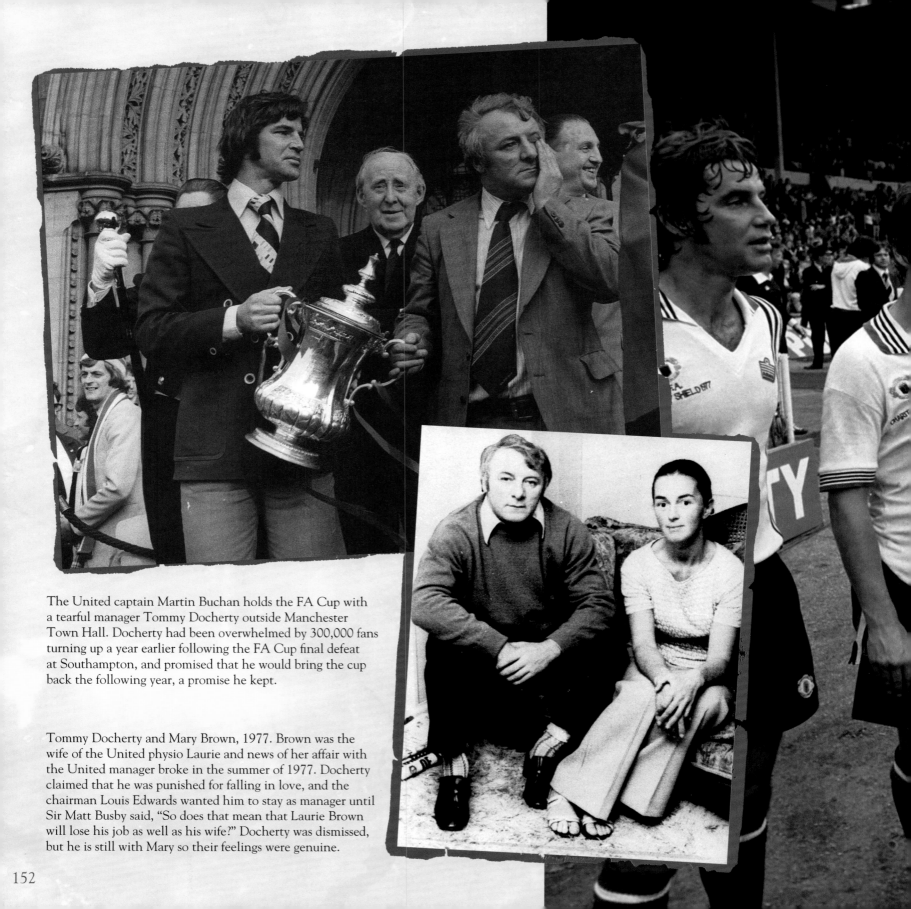

The United captain Martin Buchan holds the FA Cup with
a tearful manager Tommy Docherty outside Manchester
Town Hall. Docherty had been overwhelmed by 300,000 fans
turning up a year earlier following the FA Cup final defeat
at Southampton, and promised that he would bring the cup
back the following year, a promise he kept.

Tommy Docherty and Mary Brown, 1977. Brown was the
wife of the United physio Laurie and news of her affair with
the United manager broke in the summer of 1977. Docherty
claimed that he was punished for falling in love, and the
chairman Louis Edwards wanted him to stay as manager until
Sir Matt Busby said, "So does that mean that Laurie Brown
will lose his job as well as his wife?" Docherty was dismissed,
but he is still with Mary so their feelings were genuine.

We meet again. United and Liverpool players share the 1977 Charity Shield at Wembley. Arthur Albiston, furthest right, was just 19 when he started in the FA Cup final a few months earlier against Liverpool replacing the injured left-back Stewart Houston. According to the experts pontificating before the 1977 FA Cup final, the Scot Albiston would be United's weakest link. Efficient and industrious, he was one of United's best players in the 2-1 victory. Albiston's work ethic served him well. Only seven others have played more times for United than he has. Before leaving in 1988, he played 482 games and was the first United player to win three FA Cup winner's medals.

United line up before a Cup Winners' Cup game against French side St Etienne, September 1977. Rioting Reds inside the ground led UEFA to order United to play the return leg on a neutral ground at least 125 miles from Manchester. The decision did not prevent 31,634 United fans travelling to Devon, with the police undertaking a military-style operation to take the fans from the rail station to the ground.

Two policemen at Home Park, Plymouth, for the return leg.

155

Scottish forward Joe Jordan, signed controversially from Leeds United in January 1978, with manager Dave Sexton (right) and chairman Louis Edwards at his side.

"Leeds let Joe go over what amounted to £15 a week in wages," lamented his best friend and team-mate Gordon McQueen. "They were talking about building a new Leeds and they let Joe, one of Leeds' best young players, go to Manchester United. That was the final nail in the coffin for me and I became very disillusioned." McQueen soon followed Jordan to Old Trafford. Twenty years later, t-shirts were on sale outside Elland Road saying: "United Scum – Jordan, McQueen, Cantona and Ferdinand."

Joe Jordan made 126 United appearances and scored 41 goals for United between 1978 and 1981 before moving to Milan for £325,000. Here, he plays away at Liverpool.

"Joe is serious and to a lot of people he is dour," said team-mate Gordon McQueen. "I find him good fun. I was the best man at his wedding and he was the best man at mine. He is conscientious and a real hard grafter, someone who is totally dedicated to his work.

"Joe was the trickiest dresser at the club. He spent a few quid on his gear and still does today. As a player Joe was so determined. He had great aerial ability, timing and was quick. He was fearless too. If somebody did him then he'd do them back, absolutely no doubt. He wasn't clinical in front of goal like Ian Rush, but centre-halves hated playing against him. He was always really popular with fans, even in Milan where he wasn't a regular."

157

"I kept charging up until I ran out of grass or hit an advertising hoarding."

Defender Gordon McQueen was hugely popular with United fans, who used to chant: "Gordon McQueen, Gordon McQueen, Gordon! Gordon!" to the tune that the French sing "Allez les bleus" – especially when he made one of his runs forward.

"I love bombing forward and the crowd loved it too," McQueen said. "I kept charging up until I ran out of grass or hit an advertising hoarding. I'd run five yards with the ball and could sense that they wanted me to run a bit more. They'd really get me at it so I'd move forward even more. Managers hated it and some of the players hated it. Frank Stapleton, who was pretty serious, used to look at me and I could tell he was thinking: 'Jesus Christ, what the hell is he up to?' I did it because I used to fancy myself as a bit of a left-winger. I was always very quick too, despite being 6ft 4in with gangly legs. I was the quickest player at Leeds and I was the quickest player at Old Trafford when I arrived at the club."

Here, he is chasing Nottingham Forest's Gary Birtles, who would later sign for United in a big money move.

"Gary was under a lot of pressure," Frank Stapleton says. "In training, Gary used to score all the time and his play really flowed. He was a good player with a good engine, but he used to tense up in matches. I told him to relax. He used to wander and drop back deep. I'd say to him, 'Where are you going? Let the midfield do their job, get up here. People are criticizing you for not scoring, you are not going to score any goals from midfield.' I told him to stay up with me which he did. He broke his duck and scored 11 goals that season."

Yet Birtles did not have a future at Old Trafford.

"Gary might not agree with me, but I don't think he had the temperament to deal with the pressure of a big club," says Stapleton, a theory Bryan Robson agrees with. "He was good enough, but being good enough isn't enough for Man United. You have to be able to deal with expectation and people who have been successful for United have dealt with the continual expectation."

### LEARNING THE ROPES

"I remember going into town, a gangly 18-year-old with a few spots on my face," said Gary Bailey. "I went to a disco and not one person spoke to me all night. Girls didn't believe me when I told them that I was a goalkeeper at Manchester United."

After publication of pictures like this following his first-team debut, life changed somewhat.

"I'd always noticed the groupies hanging around the club but when I became a first-team player they were all over me," he recalled. "I remember thinking, 'Wow, I'm the man'. But then I realized that they were all over every first-team player. In discos there was a totally different response. Suddenly I was pulling the best birds around. I really had to keep my feet on the ground and bear in mind that being famous was a huge attraction to women. I had to look a bit deeper than that."

159

# The Usual Suspects

Young United fans are told to face a wall by police outside London's Euston Station in 1979, following clashes with rival Arsenal fans. This picture was used as the front cover for the book *Perry Boys*, by Ian Hough.

The
# 1980s

Without a league title since 1967, United's lack of championship honours became a drought, a problem exacerbated by the unwavering dominance of arch-rivals Liverpool. Ron Atkinson replaced Sexton and delivered attractive football and some great European nights before English clubs were banned from continental competition. Success was achieved in the FA Cup, but the league title remained elusive. The jovial showman Atkinson was replaced by Sir Alex Ferguson, an uncompromising Scot who had worked miracles for Aberdeen in Scotland. Ferguson did things his way, completely reorganizing United's football at every level. The results were not immediately obvious and there were more than a few detractors, but the foundations were laid for a bright future.

# Team Work

Every Manchester United employee, led by manager Ron Atkinson and chairman Martin Edwards, on the pitch in 1981. A similar picture taken today would have to include over 500 people.

# —LEGENDS— Bryan Robson

Bryan Robson signs for United on the pitch before a match, 1981. Alongside him are Ron Atkinson, Martin Edwards and long-time club secretary Les Olive. Robson's £1.5 million fee from West Bromwich Albion was a British transfer record.

"I knew that Liverpool and Man United had an interest in me so I told West Brom that I wanted to move on," said Robson. "I was ambitious and wanted to play for a club that was ambitious. Liverpool didn't come up with the money; they wouldn't go above £1.2million, whereas Man United went to the £1.5million, which the Albion agreed too.

"I think the fee affected me when I first went to United. Maybe I was just getting used to my team-mates, but when you come through the ranks of a football club there are no expectations. The home fans take to you because you have come through the ranks. But when you are bought as a record signing the expectations are higher from the crowd, and that means more pressure. I took time to adapt and it took another England competition, the 1982 World Cup, to get my confidence sky high again. I had a good World Cup and it proved to me that I could be one of the better players in Europe. I came back and I was flying the following season."

## FOOTBALL —STATS—

### Bryan Robson

Name: Bryan Robson

Born: 1957

Playing Career: 1974-1996

Clubs: West Bromwich Albion, Manchester United, Middlesbrough

United Appearances: 437

Goals: 99

England Appearances: 90

Goals: 26

# In Liverpool's Shadow

No matter who United signed in the early 1980s, Liverpool's domination couldn't be broken.

"Liverpool were well ahead of us, the dominant side of the early '80s," admitted Gordon McQueen. "Their recruitment was second to none and recruitment is by far the most important thing in football."

The two teams met in the 1983 Milk Cup final at Wembley. "We went a goal up through Big Norm before they scored twice. Later, I had a bit of cramp so I was shoved up front. I beat the offside trap and rounded Bruce Grobbelaar in the last minute of normal time and there wasn't a Liverpool player in sight. All I had to do was roll it into an empty net. I was going to score – there was no doubt about that – when he absolutely whacked me. I flew right up into the air. It was assault. Nowadays he would be sent off, no question."

Spot the United fans celebrating United's goal in the Liverpool end.

Norman Whiteside scores for United against Arsenal, 1983.

# —LEGENDS—

## Norman Whiteside

Norman Whiteside scores one of his most important goals for United, against Arsenal in the 1983 FA Cup semi-final at Villa Park. "Norman Whiteside was a genius of a player," said team-mate Gary Bailey. "If he had had pace he would have been one of the greatest players of all time."

> *Norman Whiteside was a genius of a player.*

## FOOTBALL —STATS—

### Norman Whiteside

Name: Norman Whiteside

Born: 1965

Playing Career: 1982-1989

Clubs: Manchester United, Everton

United Appearances: 256

Goals: 67

Northern Ireland Appearances: 38

Goals: 9

"It would have been ridiculous for us to lose to Brighton."

168

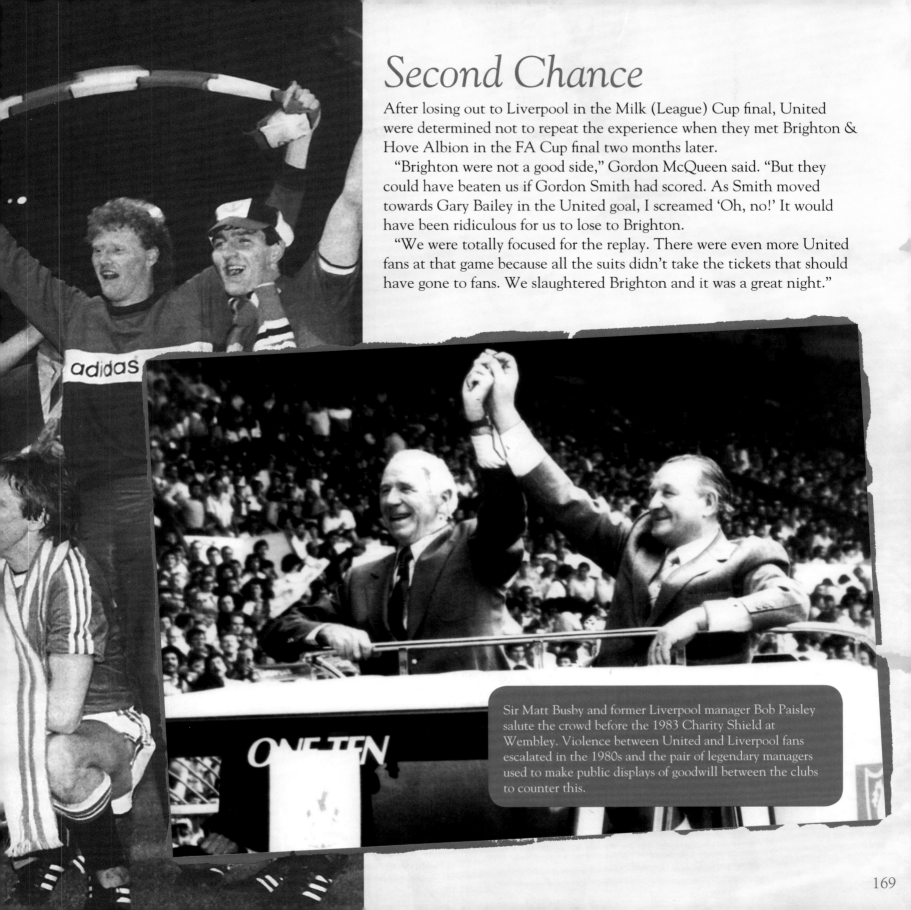

# Second Chance

After losing out to Liverpool in the Milk (League) Cup final, United were determined not to repeat the experience when they met Brighton & Hove Albion in the FA Cup final two months later.

"Brighton were not a good side," Gordon McQueen said. "But they could have beaten us if Gordon Smith had scored. As Smith moved towards Gary Bailey in the United goal, I screamed 'Oh, no!' It would have been ridiculous for us to lose to Brighton.

"We were totally focused for the replay. There were even more United fans at that game because all the suits didn't take the tickets that should have gone to fans. We slaughtered Brighton and it was a great night."

Sir Matt Busby and former Liverpool manager Bob Paisley salute the crowd before the 1983 Charity Shield at Wembley. Violence between United and Liverpool fans escalated in the 1980s and the pair of legendary managers used to make public displays of goodwill between the clubs to counter this.

> *Remi Moses was one of the hardest players I played with.*

Ron Atkinson and Mancunian midfielder Remi Moses, who followed the United manager from West Brom as part of the deal which brought Bryan Robson to Old Trafford.

"Barring Moses's desperately unlucky injury record, he would have become a clear favourite to replace Robson at the heart of the England team," remarked Atkinson.

"Remi Moses was one of the hardest players I played with," said Clayton Blackmore. "He once lashed out after Graham Hogg had kicked him in training. Except he lashed out at me and smacked me one in the jaw. I got out of the way. He was tough Remi, but I'd not done anything. I've never been one to look for fights. If I have to fight I'll fight, but he shouldn't have thrown a punch at me. He found out what had happened and he apologized."

Ron Atkinson's most extravagant foreign investment was Jesper Olsen, the Danish winger, who signed from Ajax in 1984 for £500,000.

"After an encouraging first season, Jesper looked like he would deliver huge dividends for the side," remembered Atkinson. "I figured he might develop into a contender for footballer of the year in the next season, yet his promise was undermined by serious injury. Jesper was an extremely gifted winger and a nice enough bloke, but the Danes considered him to be a fiery and explosive player. We were to find out why soon enough."

Arthur Albiston delivered Atkinson an early warning about Olsen's suspect methods on the training field within days of the Danish international's arrival.

"It's going to go off out there, gaffer, unless you watch carefully. Jesper is definitely a bit naughty," said Albiston. In the next session, Olsen made a tackle that almost wiped out Remi Moses. Big mistake, as Moses adopted his best Marvin Hagler stance and landed several blows on a terrified Olsen.

> *We did it with a certain amount of football panache and style.*

# Laid Back

Ron Atkinson relaxes in his office at The Cliff in 1984. The United manager between 1981 and 1986, Big Ron had a sunbed in an adjacent room.

"I had five years in charge at United, spent a few quid and did enough shrewd business to get most of it back," said Atkinson. "And I left United with the best record, at that time, since the great Sir Matt Busby. We never finished below the top four in the First Division, won two FA Cups and lost in the League Cup final. We were involved in European competition every year, something that had never been achieved since Matt's days.

"We also did it with a certain amount of football panache and style, living up to United's finest traditions. So it wasn't all so bad, was it?"

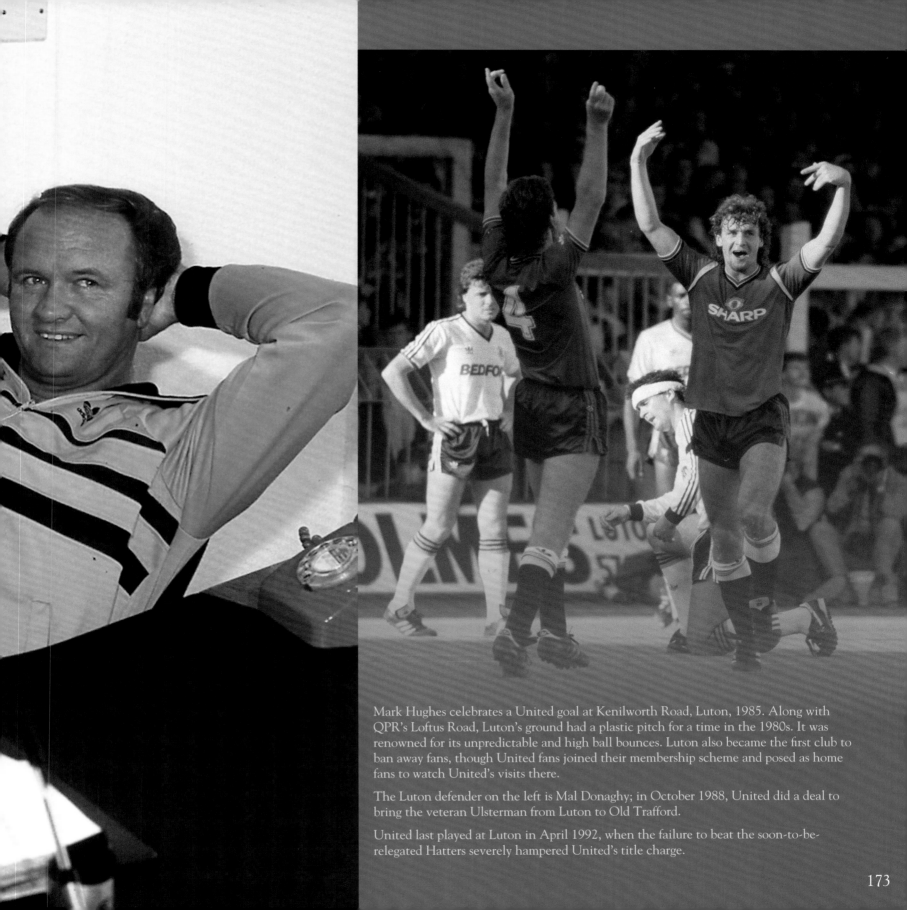

Mark Hughes celebrates a United goal at Kenilworth Road, Luton, 1985. Along with QPR's Loftus Road, Luton's ground had a plastic pitch for a time in the 1980s. It was renowned for its unpredictable and high ball bounces. Luton also became the first club to ban away fans, though United fans joined their membership scheme and posed as home fans to watch United's visits there.

The Luton defender on the left is Mal Donaghy; in October 1988, United did a deal to bring the veteran Ulsterman from Luton to Old Trafford.

United last played at Luton in April 1992, when the failure to beat the soon-to-be-relegated Hatters severely hampered United's title charge.

Everton's Peter Reid avoids United's John Gidman and Bryan Robson in the 1985 FA Cup final.

"I thought that I'd missed my chance of playing in an FA Cup final after being injured in '83," said Gidman. "We were the underdogs with Everton going for the treble and Big Ron told us, 'Don't sit back. Go at them.' It was hot and we took salt tablets. The Wembley grass was long and I used longer studs than usual. When Peter Reid hit a volley, I stretched as far as I could to reach it, convinced the ball was going in. Somehow, my stud clipped it and it went wide.

"It was a shocking decision to send Kevin Moran off and I felt for him, but we still felt confident with 10 men. With Frank Stapleton back at centre-half, we aimed for the replay until Norm the Storm did his bit and bent a winner around Neville Southall. I was the first player to congratulate him and said: 'If there wasn't 100,000 people here I'd f**k you now.' After the game, I remember picking my old Villa team-mate Andy Gray up, a tear in his eye, and telling him to keep his head up."

Bryan Robson and Frank Stapleton dispute the decision to send Kevin Moran off, while consoling the distraught Moran, 1985.

"Kevin should never have been sent off, but the referee was on his last game and wanted to make an impact," said Stapleton, who switched to centre-half when Kevin left the field.

"We still felt confident with 10 men.

Moran, the first player ever to be sent off in an FA Cup final, looks on from the bench as manager Ron Atkinson shouts instructions to his players during the 1985 match.

"People always remember you for certain things and, if you're the first to do something like getting sent off in an FA Cup final, naturally you're going to be remembered more for that than anything else," recalled Moran.

"People ask me if I'm bothered about it, thinking it's something that hangs over me. That's not the case. I celebrated that evening no different from any of the other players."

United beat Everton 1-0 with an extra-time goal from Norman Whiteside.

Moran's reaction changes as Norman Whiteside scores.

United lift the 1985 FA Cup. Left to right: captain Bryan Robson with the trophy, Gary Bailey, John Gidman, Gordon Strachan, Norman Whiteside, Paul McGrath, Arthur Albiston, and Mark Hughes.

United's goalscoring hero Norman Whiteside raises a glass of champagne after leaving the team coach following the 1985 FA Cup final. Whiteside was not adverse to a tipple.

# Head For Heights

After winning the FA Cup, United started the 1985-6 season with 10 straight league victories. A first league title since 1967 seemed possible as teams such as rivals Manchester City were beaten 3-0 away. Irish-born defender Paul McGrath, here out-jumping City's Mancunian striker Mark Lillis, was one of United's best performers before injuries hampered United's form.

"It was our best chance to win the league with United," said defender John Gidman. "I don't know why, whether it was nerves, but it wasn't the manager's fault. It was such a shame we couldn't give fans the one trophy they wanted."

United's ever-reliable defender Mike Duxbury poses, inexplicably, with two puppies in 1986.

> "We couldn't give the fans the one trophy they wanted."

> **"** *Muhren was a superb technician who made a revolutionary impact on our game.* **"**

Check out the haircuts of the United players as they go for a run around Salford. Arnold Muhren has his eyes closed in the centre.

"The Dutchman was blessed with a well-proven creative ability and played wide on the left," said his manager Ron Atkinson. "It was a position I had always found hard to solve. He was heaven sent and came on a free.

"I don't think Arnold ever collected the credit he deserved from United's followers. Yet he was a superb technician who made a revolutionary impact on our game with his total football education. He helped Robson no end in the art of passing. Arnie didn't have to pass to feet, not when he could cause more destruction by passing into space. People used to have an image of Arnie as a laid-back, maybe even lazy, strolling type of player. Far from it. He was a highly competitive trainer, a complete football nut, and never out of the top three in any of our training runs. When he left, I wanted him to stay another couple of years. But Johan Cruyff, his own hero, lured him to Ajax."

The United players in Manchester Airport in 1985 with the back-permed hairstyles which were popular at the time. Billy Garton is in the centre with the holdall. A United fan from Ordsall in Salford, he used to catch a bus to Old Trafford, even when he was a first-teamer. His career was cut short by chronic fatigue syndrome, before he retrained as a teacher. He now runs a successful football coaching academy in California.

> "I've got a dog called Charlie, Mr Chairman, but I thought we were talking cars."

United manager Ron Atkinson with his new Mercedes car at The Cliff training ground, January 1986.

"Martin Edwards pointed out that my predecessor, Dave Sexton, had a Rover," recalled Atkinson. "Well, I've got a dog called Charlie, Mr Chairman, but I thought we were talking cars.' On the spot he agreed to replace the car I already had, a Mercedes coupé, for an up-to-date model."

This was Atkinson's second Merc. Ten months after this photo, he was dismissed and replaced by Sir Alex Ferguson.

# Determined Stance

Sir Alex Ferguson with his players at The Cliff on his first morning as manager of Manchester United, November 1986. Clayton Blackmore was in Ferguson's first match line-up at Oxford United.

"It was nice to play in the first game under Alex, even though we lost," commented Blackmore. "He spoke to me in the week leading up to the game about what he was going to do. But his accent was so broad that I couldn't understand a word of what he was saying to me. I just nodded because I really wanted to do well for him. "Alex's man management is as good as can be. He has made mistakes, but he's achieved at the highest level for years." Blackmore has other memories of Ferguson. "Alex and assistant Archie Knox would play head tennis at The Cliff. We always tried to avoid being dragged in as referee because you'd end up getting punished either way. If you were ref when the manager lost he'd have you running outside."

# True Colours

Sir Alex Ferguson on his first day as Manchester United manager, 1986. Tabloid newspaper photographers often carried scarves and hats to liven up otherwise dull settings. Ferguson is all smiles here at The Cliff, but his battles to reorganize United at every level were only just beginning.

Sir Alex Ferguson with Gordon Strachan and Jim Leighton, who had both played under him at Aberdeen. Strachan's transfer to Old Trafford before Ferguson joined was complicated. "When Gordon Strachan dropped in to play a testimonial game for Martin Buchan I got the vibe that he might be on his way from Aberdeen," said manager Ron Atkinson. "You could detect the friction, even at a long range, between him and Fergie. He, apparently, believed that, although Gordon was only 27, he had been flying down the wing on just one trip too many. Fergie considered him burnt out with nothing left in the legs. My judgement was that Strachan was worth signing for United at a price of £500,000. There was just one snag – he had already taken it upon himself to sign for what appeared to be half the clubs in Europe as well."

United paid £70,000 to one such club, FC Koln of Germany, to free Strachan from a pre-contract agreement that carried his name. In his first season, 1984-5, Strachan scored 15 league goals. "Sure, a fair few were penalties, but then he won plenty of them as well. He got so overexposed in TV playbacks that revealed his technique, it blew Strach's mind and he started missing them. He had, it's true, earned himself a reputation as a rag doll merchant, but for me he made the most of his attacking opportunities. When that now famously recorded 10-point lead went down the pan it was tied to a dislocated shoulder suffered by Strachan when he collided with a post at West Brom. In roughly three years at United he always looked to be in the very place he was born to play." Those United fans who watched him score the equalizer at Anfield in 1988, before smoking an imaginary cigar in front of the Kop, will not disagree.

Ferguson let Strachan go once again – to Leeds where he was in the side which pipped United to the 1992 league title. Leighton was famously dropped by Ferguson after a suspect performance in the 1990 FA Cup final. Les Sealey played in the replay and Leighton never spoke to Ferguson again.

Vinny Jones heads a goal against United at Wimbledon's old Plough Lane ground in 1989. With a mostly terraced capacity of just over 10,000, United were often uncomfortable in these dilapidated surroundings on which Wimbledon conversely thrived. Jones, a former hod carrier on a building site, had joined Wimbledon from a non-league side and became an integral part of their Crazy Gang alongside Dennis Wise, with whom he is clashing to score this goal.

Mark Hughes scores for United's only goal in a 5-1 defeat by Manchester City at Maine Road in September 1989. United's expensive new signings, Gary Pallister, Paul Ince, and Danny Wallace, were humiliated by a City side seemingly short on quality. Ferguson said after that game that he went to bed hoping never to wake up, but has since overseen convincing victories over City, revenge coming when an Andrei Kanchelskis-inspired United side beat City 5-0 on Bonfire Night, 1994.

# Before the
# PREMIER
# LEAGUE

United started the '90s with a sizeable number of fans calling for Sir Alex Ferguson to be sacked. On the face of it, the club seemed further away from winning the league title than ever and average gates slipped below 40,000. Ferguson's first trophy, the 1990 FA Cup, bought him time and European Cup Winners' Cup success in Rotterdam a year later, hero status. United narrowly missed out on the 1992 league title to Leeds, but the signing of Eric Cantona later that year from United's Yorkshire rivals was heralded as the final piece in a jigsaw which would see United lift the league championship trophy after a 26-year wait. United were changing just as football as a whole was undergoing seismic change.

" *The final piece in the jigsaw.* "

" McClair still wonders why he
wasn't sent off.

## The Battle of Old Trafford

The tabloid press called it "The Battle of Old Trafford" after United striker Brian McClair and Arsenal's Nigel Winterburn (on the ground) were involved in a prolonged fracas on the Old Trafford turf during a tense league game in 1990-1. McClair still wonders to this day why he was not sent off for his behaviour. Both teams had points deducted, though Arsenal still went on to win the league. Nigel Winterburn was on the receiving end of colourful chants from United fans for the rest of his career.

A quiet and reserved figure in the dressing-room, Mark Hughes underwent a transformation on the pitch into an aggressive, powerful, yet skilful centre-forward. One of the few players ever to return to Old Trafford, his sale to Barcelona after scoring 24 goals in his first full season, caused anger on the terraces at the loss of such a dazzling young prospect. When he was bought back by Sir Alex Ferguson, he demonstrated his range of striking skills, from powerful headers to his athletic volleying. Hughes, the possessor, according to his ex-Barça colleague Gary Lineker, of 'the strongest ankles in football', soaked up much punishment from defenders while holding up the ball to great effect. "Sparky" was the scorer of many important, season-defining goals, often dragging United back from the brink of defeat. Here, he's just scored in the 1990 FA Cup final against Crystal Palace. In 1995, he left to join Chelsea, where he became the only twentieth-century player to win four FA Cup medals, and, until he joined Manchester City in 2008, managed at international and club level with distinction.

"

*The scorer of many important, season-defining goals.*

"

# Half Measures

United and Liverpool players share the 1990 Charity Shield at Wembley. Margaret Thatcher was still in power and it was the last time Liverpool were crowned champions. United met them after winning the FA Cup. Today, the traditional pre-season opener is decided by a penalty shoot-out but, then, the honours were divided.

Danny Wallace signed for United in a £1.2 million deal in September 1989, initially joining fellow new recruits Gary Pallister and Paul Ince in Manchester's Ramada Hotel; Wallace brought his family and their dog, a Rottweiler.

Wallace scored key goals in United's 1989-90 cup run at Newcastle in the fifth round and in the semi-final against Oldham.

Here, Tottenham's Paul Gascoigne watches on as Wallace volleys the ball at White Hart Lane. Wallace was diagnosed with multiple sclerosis in 1995, the disease curtailing his football career at the age of 31.

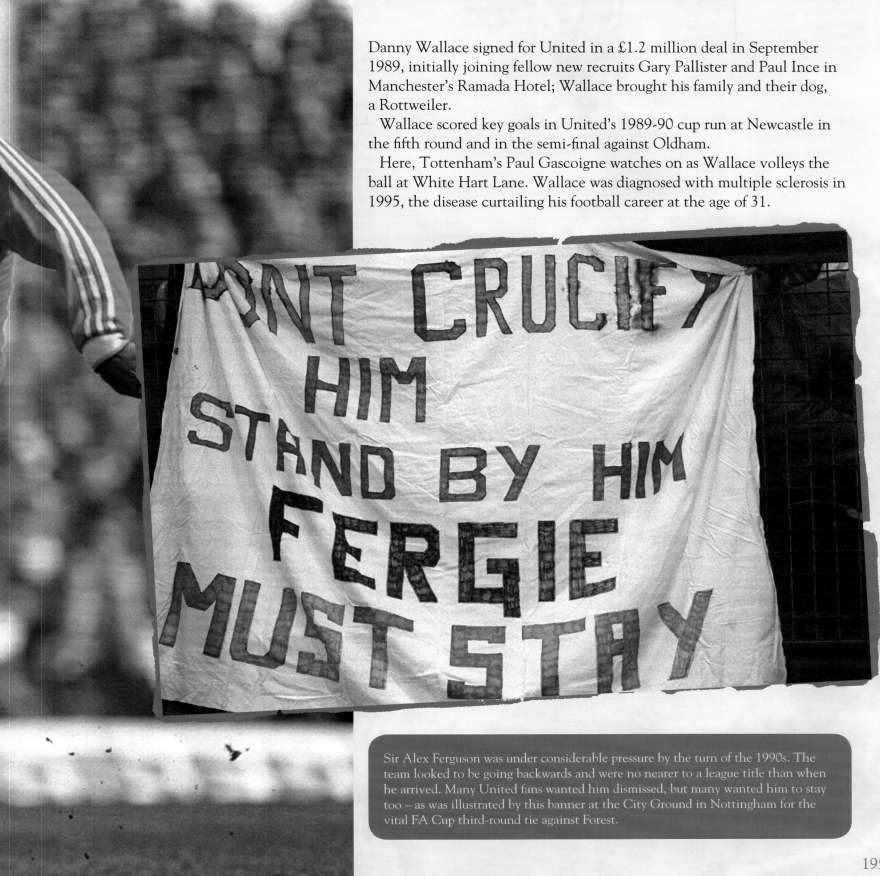

Sir Alex Ferguson was under considerable pressure by the turn of the 1990s. The team looked to be going backwards and were no nearer to a league title than when he arrived. Many United fans wanted him dismissed, but many wanted him to stay too – as was illustrated by this banner at the City Ground in Nottingham for the vital FA Cup third-round tie against Forest.

Striker Mark Robins is often described as the man who saved Sir Alex Ferguson. The locally born forward struck the only goal in a hard to win FA Cup third-round tie at Nottingham Forest in January 1990. A momentum began to build which led to United winning the cup, Ferguson's first trophy as United manager.

> *The man who saved Sir Alex Ferguson.*

Steve Bruce in Warsaw, 1991, ahead of United's European Cup Winners' Cup semi-final against Legia Warsaw.

With Lee Sharpe as man of the match, United ran out comfortable winners to set up a final against Barcelona. It was United's first season in Europe following the five-year ban on English clubs following the Heysel Stadium disaster, and the spectacle of European football didn't completely catch on. United's home games that season were against Pecsi Munkas, Wrexham, Montpellier and Legia Warsaw and saw attendances of just 28,411, 29,405, 41,942, and 44,269.

# Singing in the Rain

United reached the European Cup Winners' Cup final against Barcelona in 1991. Authorities were nervous about 26,000 Reds crossing the Channel to the Dutch port, especially with 14,000 Barça fans added to the mix.

To limit the potential for disorder, fans initially had to book on officially organized coaches or planes – until the club relented and issued 7,000 tickets to independent travellers, most of whom headed to Amsterdam.

What the authorities didn't understand was that with the "blissed-up Madchester" music scene at its peak, creating disorder wouldn't be a priority for many Reds. There was also a point to prove that United fans could behave abroad.

The venue, Feyenoord's De Kuip (the bowl), is now the most popular stadium in Holland. Yet in 1991 three of its stands remained uncovered – hardly ideal given the unrelenting rain on the day of the final. The rain could have made an uninviting Rotterdam depressing, but United fans were used to downpours and partied away, singing Madchester anthems like *Sit Down* by James.

> *United fans were used to downpours and partied away.*

Fortune favoured United in Rotterdam, as Mark Hughes scored twice against Barcelona, the club that had disposed of him – the second a fierce volley from an implausible angle that, according to Sir Alex Ferguson, "left their goalkeeper picking daisies somewhere". So overjoyed was the United manager after the final whistle that he impersonated the conductor of an orchestra, with the soddened fans singing: *Always look on the bright side of life*.

> "
> *A fierce volley left their goalkeeper picking daisies somewhere.*
> "

LEFT TO RIGHT: Paul Ince, Lee Sharpe, Gary Pallister (with the European Cup Winners' Cup), Les Sealey, Mike Phelan, Steve Bruce, Clayton Blackmore, Brian McClair, and Bryan Robson celebrate on the podium.

Blackmore had kicked a shot from Michael Laudrup off the line with only a few minutes left. "It was Clayton's finest moment in a red jersey," said Sir Alex Ferguson. "As long as there is a Manchester United, that rescue act will be remembered."

"Brucey lost the ball and he still thanks me," explained Blackmore, "I was just there on the line." United held on for victory.

“It was Clayton's finest moment in a red jersey.

”

United's young winger Lee Sharpe sets out on a run against Barcelona in the 1991 European Cup Winners' Cup final. Signed for £185,000 from Fourth Division Torquay United, Birmingham-born Sharpe burst onto the scene in 1988 and stayed at Old Trafford until 1996, when he moved to Leeds United for a fee of more than £4 million.

Hugely popular with United fans, Sharpe retired from football well before his 30th birthday – a decision he never regretted. He enjoys his life and has been a star in several reality television programmes.

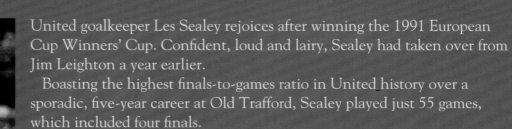

United goalkeeper Les Sealey rejoices after winning the 1991 European Cup Winners' Cup. Confident, loud and lairy, Sealey had taken over from Jim Leighton a year earlier.

Boasting the highest finals-to-games ratio in United history over a sporadic, five-year career at Old Trafford, Sealey played just 55 games, which included four finals.

He died in 2001, aged just 43, after suffering a heart attack while working as West Ham's goalkeeping coach.

Darren Ferguson and Denis Irwin during Ferguson's debut against Sheffield United in 1991, just before his 18th birthday. A midfielder, Ferguson was a regular at the start of the 1992-3 season, before a hamstring injury hampered his progress. Although the other players respected his ability, it was awkward for him with his father being manager, and once Roy Keane joined the club, Ferguson junior featured less and was sold to Wolves in 1994. Like his father, Ferguson always wanted to be a manager and he had a great start at Peterborough United.

Ryan Giggs wears a Russian hat in Moscow's Red Square, prior to the UEFA Cup game against Torpedo Moscow in 1991-2. United were eliminated on penalties.

It was United's first game against Russian opposition. In the Old Trafford first leg – a fixture which marked United's 50th home European tie – United were surprisingly held to a 0-0 draw in front of a rather meagre 19,998 crowd. Thanks to UEFA regulations, manager Sir Alex Ferguson could only play three non-English players and two "assimilated" players. In reality, this meant that he could not select nine players from his first-team squad, breaking up a team which had won five successive Premiership games without conceding a goal.

The author would like to thank Joyce Woolridge, the lads at Mirrorpix in Watford, David and Fergus at *The Mirror*, Captain Derrick Kemp for sharing my enthusiasm of bygone eras, agent Paul Moreton for bringing the project together, Richard Havers, editor Elizabeth Stone, proofreader Rebecca Ellis and designer Kevin Gardner. And, of course, the lovely Ba for not considering me an oddball as I sifted through 10,000 Manchester United images.